The History of
VANITY

D1517935

The History of
VANITY

John Woodforde

ST. MARTIN'S PRESS · New York

Copyright © John Woodforde, 1992

First published in the United States of America in 1992

All rights reserved. For information, write:
Scholarly and Reference Division,
St. Martin's Press Inc. · 175 Fifth Avenue
New York · NY 10010

ISBN 0-312-08605-9

Library of Congress Cataloging in Publication Data

Woodforde, John
  The history of vanity/John Woodforde.
    p. cm
  0-312-08605-9
  1. Pride and vanity—History. 2. Beauty,
  Personal—History.
  I. Title.
  BJ 1535.P9W66 1922
  177'.4–dc20   92–17622
                                                       CIP

Printed in Great Britain

Contents

List of Illustrations

Acknowledgements

John Woodforde is grateful to Peter Clifford for the idea and to his daughters Catherine and Sophie for their help.

Introduction

Narcissus of the old Greek story was there at the beginning. He fell in love with his own beauty, admired continually his reflection in a pool, failed to eat and died. Oscar Wilde's youthful Dorian Gray became more and more enamoured of his appearance and spent hours in a locked room admiring his fair young face in a mirror. He too died of his own volition as a portrait of him seemed to change for the worse. Where this element of narcissism creeps in, beyond the bounds of self respect, it seems vanity begins.

Narcissus and Dorian Gray were vain indeed. So was Sir Walter Elliot in Jane Austen's *Persuasion*, but he managed to keep going. 'Vanity was the beginning and end of Sir Walter Elliot's character: vanity of person and of situation. Few women could think more of their personal appearance than he did . . . he considered the blessing of beauty as inferior only to the blessing of a baronetcy.'

Richmal Crompton's Robert Brown, brother of William, was vain-pathetic. Distant during a family conference, he 'stands in front of the mantelpiece studying his reflection in the mirror and trying to solve the eternal problem of whether he is good-looking or not'.[1] Wodehouse's Bertie Wooster is vain-resolute, lying in bed and discussing with Jeeves his clothes and accessories for a day of sauntering ease. Another person may be vain-athletic, wearing a track suit for tea and picking up a tennis racquet for a snapshot in the garden. Several people in 1991 even went as far as having silicone injections in the arm to make their muscles look more impressive.

But for thousands of men there is a wild-man type of vanity, springing from an urge implanted by education and custom, to prove their masculinity – in a way that women do not feel about their femininity. They set themselves perilous tasks on mountains, play dangerous games and have appalling accidents. Even the squash court is a well-known scene of injury. Although in history men were long happy with so-called feminine adornments, such as elaborate hats and buttons, and clothes of sharply different colours, and with sweet-smelling lotions (until the 1820s in modern western societies), their instinct has been for many years to deny themselves such things and to show how male they are: they may not annihilate a friend on a squash court but a slight injury there is not too unusual.

The vanity of such Roman emperors as Augustus and Commodus (the latter was disagreeably vain about everything, especially his virility) was exploited for publicity purposes, and statues distributed for copying throughout the Empire showed inspiring young heads on bodies that were not their own but those of athletes.

Augustus was plain, according to a handed-down description by Suetonius. His sculptors transformed him as they entered into a propaganda drive he ordered. The Prima Porta sculpture presents him as a Greek idealized figure, the pose copied from that of a spear bearer carved in the early fourth century BC. That statue was naked, but Augustus preached moral-

Oscar Wilde aged twenty-eight. In later life he was said to look furtive. This was because of his habit of covering his bad teeth with a hand in front of his mouth

ity and insisted on clothes. In his work the sculptor implies an impressive physique by making Augustus' armour fit in such a way that a splendidly modelled torso is suggested.

Commodus liked to portray himself as Hercules: one portrait depicts him draped in a lion skin and carrying a hero's club. His hair, heavily drilled in the stone, contrasts with a polished skin. The canny sculptor, no doubt aware of his client's unattractive vanity, has contrived to capture a degree of official dignity while at the same time hinting at sadism and effeminacy (according to Gibbon, Commodus had an outsize seraglio of both sexes).[2]

In the days before cameras vain people delighted in having their portraits painted, especially under their own direction. The seventeenth-century Lord Herbert of Cherbury, pyrotechnically vain in his autobiography, saw to it, according to David Piper in *The English Face*, that the portraits of him fully brought out his beauty: he is shown melancholic as he lies prostrate by a stream, lovelorn in a lacey shirt and so grand in profile as to seem an emperor.

The apparent body vanity and pomposity of many late Victorians, as shown in photographs, is in fact less due to vainglory than to the way images were made. Exposures might last sixty seconds. 'Give a man enough time to know that he is being recorded for posterity,' writes Thelma Chapman, 'and he will invariably smooth his hair and assume a noble posture'.[3]

For a woman, being vain has always been taken seriously, according to a recent article in a woman's magazine.

Lord Herbert of Cherbury, a poseur and unusually vain. The seventeenth-century artist is unknown

Vanity has its roots in insecurity and its crown in greedy dreams . . . To be vain is to watch for faults with a nervy vigilance which excludes other people. Obsessive vanity can kill intimacy; tell your lover with sobs that you look horrible and he may believe you . . . Vanity is not a vice but an affliction. An ordinary-looking person without vanity can look very good, but a handsome woman troubled with vanity is hag-ridden.[4]

Some kinds of vanity are of course ridiculous, but all are aware of being in one way or another a little vain. After middle age, men tend to be vainer than women: they pull hair down over the forehead and wear jackets cut to hide a paunch; they jog; they drive cars, and also mowing machines, rather fast. Elderly male

Walking dress for Hyde Park, 1797. Vanity could make a person look ridiculous

voices are sometimes trained by elocutionists to sound younger on the telephone. But if they feel better for taking trouble with appearances and are more pleasing and impressive to others, where is the harm?

If a person is vain about his house and wants to show everyone round, what does it matter? (A glaring exception must be Hermann Goering, conducting tours of his Hitler-approved residence, whose oil paintings had been appropriated from museums.)[5] Does it matter that many like the status of living in old houses with history rather than in new houses? If vanity crops up it is hardly in a form anyone could object to.

There may be the question of one's name. Some people desire a double-barrelled surname or find that a slight alteration in spelling can work wonders. There are several ways of making the name Smith look more distinctive, and Trollope's ambitious clergyman, born Slop, 'added an "e" for the sake of euphony'.[6]

Vain-reckless is a term that could be used when the poor-sighted inconvenience themselves and others by going without spectacles. The eighteenth-century Parson Woodforde had a friend, 'very advanced in years', who did this, driving a single-horse chaise although unable to 'see the ruts distinctly'. The late Rex Harrison thought it effete to let a woman drive him and refused, because of his image as an actor, to be photographed with the spectacles necessary for him to drive safely. If the Press was about, he would drive his Rolls Royce almost unseeingly until out of view.[7]

At all times people have been said to be recklessly vain when efforts to improve appearances went wrong: when faces were ruined by putting on white lead; stout women became ill from doing up their stays too tight and hair turned green from attempts to hide greyness. It may or may not be vain to sunbathe, which is a pleasant sensation, but it must surely be vain to paint oneself with a colour to give the look of a healthy sun tan.

Vanity about age takes several forms. People make a secret of their age, minimize it and then when old boast about it, even exaggerating it to be told they have worn well (but they should not boast too much: the *Guiness Book of Records* is vigilant over claims of age and observes: 'No single subject is more obscured by vanity and deceit than extreme longevity'). Everyone's sensitivity is reflected in the way newspapers report people's ages, knowing that readers will think of their own and for a moment compare.

Over the years there has been much vanity to do with teeth. The strikingly mechanical appearance of late Georgian false teeth, coupled with their disappearance just before meals, made their acquisition an event that could hardly go unremarked. Contemporary memoirs indicate that plenty of half-admiring comments were sometimes made. Men did not seem to mind taking their false teeth out at meal times, but women struggled not to do so. Their bother with slipping teeth lay behind the Victorian vanity of eating sandwiches in the bedroom just before dinner. It was a custom which partially insured against dental disaster at the table as well as making possible the affectation that young ladies lived on air, or at any rate did not possess anything so gross as a healthy appetite.

Vanity in one or other of its aspects is a condition which, as has been said, affects everyone. The dictionary seems to dwell on dandies and defines vanity with references to triviality, futility and conceit and

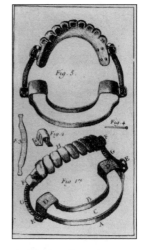

An eighteenth-century sprung device for decorating a toothless upper jaw when no lower teeth were missing. These teeth were useless for mastication

the empty people of Bunyan's town called Vanity. But according to a line in Congreve's *The Way of the World*, 'true vanity is in the power of pleasing'.[8] Taken in this sense vanity could amount to nobility, as where a defect is hidden for the comfort of others as well as oneself. According to some any kind of vanity should nearly always be accepted, as Lord Chesterfield tells his son, of whom he requests

> a complaisant indulgence for people's weaknesses, and innocent, though ridiculous vanities. If a man has a mind to be thought wiser, or a woman handsomer, than they really are, their error is a comfortable one to themselves, and an innocent one with

Philip Dormer Stanhope, 4th Earl of Chesterfield and author of *Letters to his Son*. Painted when aged seventy-one by Allan Ramsay

regard to other people; and I would rather make them my friends by indulging them in it, than my enemies by endeavouring (and that to no purpose) to undeceive them.

Erasmus, writing a century earlier, said something similar in *De Civilitate*, 1526: 'It is part of the highest civility if, while never erring yourself, you ignore the errors of others'. In 1529 Baldassar Castiglione's *The Book of the Courtier*, famous as the best guide for young members of the English establishment, there is advice on how to flatter the vanity of one's masters and of the ladies.

The present book considers the path of a word whose meaning wavers between good and bad. Precision is impossible. Is it good or arrogant to radically improve one's face, to boast a little, to pronounce words in a certain way? It could be one or the other. Always, too, there is collective vanity, calling people to so behave and dress as to keep in step with others in their group.

It can hardly be culpable to please by dressing suitably, and looking and smelling clean. That is self-respect. And who could criticize for over-decoration the late seventeenth-century daughters of impoverished aristocrats? They badly needed husbands and were in competition with City merchants' daughters on offer with big dowries. 'Ours are commodities lying on our hands,' a humble country gentleman wrote sadly in 1668.[9]

As for men, generalizations about their vanity in trying always to seem masculine and dominant have become confused since the 1950s by a tendency to be softer and more gentle, however sport-loving. The situation is barely clarified by the massively-selling

book of 1990, *Iron John* by Robert Bly. Mr Bly, a poet
with rather long white hair, superintends the Men's
Movement in America and holds courses. In the
1950s, he says, in a rather specious book, the man was
one-sidedly male, but since then he has tended to pay
more attention to his feminine side and to be more
thoughtful.

'He's a nice boy who pleases not only his mother
but also the young woman he is living with.' Mr Bly
thinks this philosophy has all gone too far among
'most contemporary men': 'There is something wonderful about men welcoming their feminine consciousness, but many are not happy . . . You quickly
notice the lack of energy in them. They are life-pre-
serving but not exactly life-giving.'

Mr Bly would like a degree of male sexual vanity to
reassert itself, believing that receptivity has not been
enough to carry marriages through recent times: 'In
every relationship something *fierce* is needed once in a
while: both men and women need to have it.'

To encourage young men to be properly firm and
masculine fathers, Mr Bly gets members of his classes
to hug other members as if they were babies needing
comfort. Several consented to be photographed for an
August 1991 issue of *The Independent Magazine*.

If the behaviour of men may be subject to their vanity, there is no doubt that false hair is sometimes considered an article of over-decoration and of vanity.
False teeth, however, once they became efficient, were
soon accepted as articles of necessity. The modern
kind could have helped the unfortunate Oscar Wilde,
who has been described as looking oddly furtive
while telling his jokes. He looked furtive because he
was ashamed of his teeth and put a hand in front of
them.[10] America's President Grant found himself

unable to address the crowds during his world cruise because his denture was swept overboard as he sunbathed, and Winston Churchill's war speeches would have been too slurred to rally the nation without a partial front set made by a dentist later knighted.[11]

Dubious vanity presents itself where there is narcissism: sensual gratification from one's own body. The mythical story of Narcissus, mentioned already, has been written up as follows:

> Narcissus was so beautiful that many lovers, both men and women courted him, but he repulsed them all. Then the Nymph Echo fell in love with him . . . Narcissus ignored her and she wasted away to a mere voice. The youth, however, was eventually requited for his cruelty. A lover rejected by him prayed to Nemesis, who condemned Narcissus to the contemplation of his own beauty reflected in a pool on Mount Helicon. The more he looked, the deeper he fell in love with himself. This futile passion held him in its grip, as he lay day after day beside the pool, until he withered and died. The gods turned him into the narcissus flower.

Many who do not much look in mirrors nevertheless contrive to stamp their image on things they own. Narcissism can be evident in people who have formed considerable collections of beautiful objects from the past; their kind of vanity is quickly suspected and becomes obvious as they begin to show you round. They are seeing their acquisitions, it is realized, more as a personal statement reflecting their taste and style than as a tribute to those whose artefacts they have assembled. Connoisseurship at any level may well be an act of vanity, just as the enthusiasm of those who paint their walls in unexpected colours may be. Interior decoration can seem to be a form of vanity. 'All it comes down to,' says Nicholas Haslam, a professional exponent, 'is making a setting in which people look prettier.' And it is perhaps vanity that sells the magazines which demonstrate the sought-after state.[12]

In 1990 there was an exhibition in London's Serpentine Gallery which mocked narcissism, the American artist Barbara Bloom going for it with no holds barred. Using the language of eighteenth-century *vanitas* representations the exhibition room made an almost claustrophobic visualization of self-love, a comic response to the personality cult attracted by artists. She ironically presented four battered, antique-like busts of herself, cameo brooches of her face, delicate cups showing her profile beneath, and chocolates moulded in the form of her features. Chairs of eighteenth-century design sported on their covers profiles of Miss Bloom's head and little motifs of her signature. One chair was astonishingly decorated with obviously authentic reproductions of X-rays of Miss Bloom's teeth. There was also a range of looking glasses.

The looking glass is an article of furniture which has attracted several writers. Virginia Woolf begins a story called *The Lady in the Looking Glass*: 'People should not leave looking glasses hanging in their rooms'. Jane Austen wrote of all 'the large looking glasses' in the dressing-room of Sir Walter Elliot. They were an unusual luxury until the end of Elizabeth I's reign. The vanity of the queen – she even painted veins on her brow to simulate youthful translucency – influenced court furnishings, and personal appearance was so important that trade in glass mirrors increased. Metal mirrors for the pocket were still in use in Elizabethan times, courtiers finding them an important item in their equipment.

Vanity of behaviour has been almost unpleasant when it went with stupidity and illiteracy, as in the case of those former country gentlemen whose only concern in life was to cut a good figure in the chase. Their fame was 'on the field of pleasure, not the field of battle,' said Defoe. There are plenty of sports today in which participants show a similar vanity, even swimming and jogging.

Feelings of vanity may occasionally be noticed in the behaviour of certain men who are small. They try to stand on things. Yul Brynner the film actor was short and in one exterior scene – in 'The Magnificent Seven' – he built himself a little mound of earth so that he would look as tall as Steve McQueen. The latter responded by casually kicking at the mound each time he passed thus reducing Mr Brynner's height.

1

Disgusting Dress and Disguise

It used to be said around 1900 by health campaigners that the women of ancient Greece had ideal figures without needing corsets, but to meet collective vanity Greek women were indeed corseted. And the treatment began at birth. To promote a good shape infants were so swaddled that neither arms nor legs had independent motion until six months old. When girls became adolescent Greek mothers tightened woollen bands round their torsos to keep them slender, and if this did not work the girls were just given less to eat.[1]

Altering the shape of the female form, reducing this part and adding to that has always been practised. Breasts through the ages have suffered for the sake of vanity, during the 1920s being compressed to the point of obliteration; in modern times they have been surgically enlarged. Elsewhere fatty tissue has been squeezed into a new shape by lacing. An extreme kind of fat removal, produced by slimmers not eating, manifests itself in the illness of anorexia nervosa.

The oddest female vanity must be the ancient Chinese treatment of girls' feet. These were tightly bound to make them small and cause protective feelings in males. The procedure, which went on in China well into the twentieth century, was at first an upper class fashion. It spread to all but the very poor – who needed women as well as men for work.

When the girls were about seven, their feet were wrapped in strips of cloth, bending all but the big toe

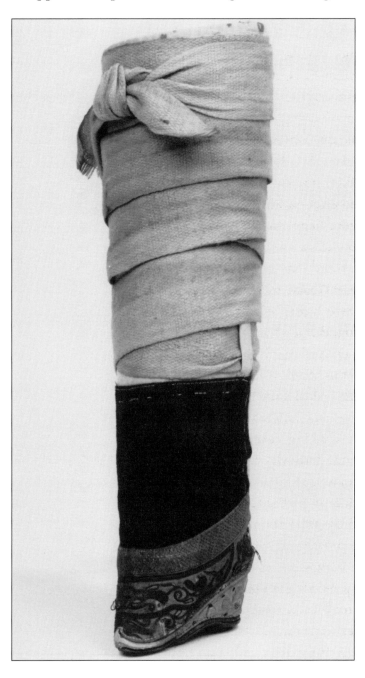

A device for reducing a Chinese girl's foot to a size considered pleasing to men

beneath the sole of the foot. A block of wood was bandaged under the heel to give the girl limited, stiff-legged movement. Once the feet became suitably deformed she had to keep on the bindings to move at all. Even in provocative Chinese paintings, nudes are seen wearing their foot-bindings.[2] Damage to the feet of English girls, on a much smaller scale, was brought about in the late eighteenth century by the dead straight shoe which had no heel and made no differentiation between the left or right foot. Again there was the notion that difficulty in walking would make men feel protective.

In trying to present their bodies to best advantage men have long hankered after padding for the shoulders and exposure of good legs, and vanity was the reason for what might be called the male mini-skirt of the Middle Ages. This tunic skirt, from being knee length in 1340, rose by 1360 to the mid-thigh and then to the hips. Beneath were tight-fitting hose in two parts crudely fastened together at the top.

The Church never ceased to disapprove and Chaucer's Parson in *The Canterbury Tales* said this of the young male wearers: 'Alas! some of them show the very boss of the privy member and pushed out parts that look like the malady of hernia in the wrapping of their hose, and the buttocks of such persons look like the hind parts of an ape.'[3]

Some men of the Middle Ages thought masculinity should be demonstrated even further and padded out their chests and seats to produce an S shape. An awkwardness at the crotch between the hose led to the invention of the boldly projecting codpiece to fit over the genitals. Despite troublesome adjustment with laces, men came to wear their codpieces with pride; some of these were colourfully decorated and some,

Fourteenth-century young men in brief tunic skirts and tight hose. This illustration from *The Decameron* shows Boccaccio and others in retreat from the plague

in the Spanish manner, were specially stuffed upright to suggest virility. They had a protective function, of course, as well as showing maleness, and armourers turned out a metal kind with a useful hinge at the top. The end of the codpiece came with wider breeches worn with much padding similar to women's wide farthingales, and the codpiece disappeared into their bulk.[4]

The peascod belly of the sixteenth century was perhaps the most absurd of the male vanities; it consisted of a doublet shaped and stuffed to give the impression of a small pointed paunch.[5] At around this time

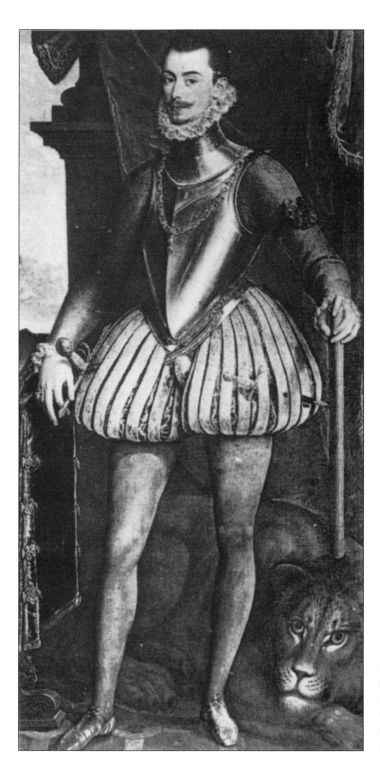

Don Juan of Austria in the seventeenth century. Breeches had become wider than previously, but the cod piece was still allowed to show women, too, liked the suggestion of a paunch, leaning back and pushing out their fronts. Low necklines came in with the liberation of the Renaissance, but before long it was decreed that women should be fully covered, especially their bosoms. After about 1615 a general plumpness was required with hips artificially rounded. Then came a long period of struggles for a slender silhouette, with corsets and with high heels (to increase the apparent length of legs). In the late eighteenth century almost bare bosoms became usual again for all, and a lot of piled-up hair.

The specially stuffed doublet of the peascod belly

The complicated fashionable clothes of the eighteenth century encouraged much vain behaviour (some account of dandy dress is given in Chapter 4). A woman, according to a lady's maid writing to the *Spectator* in 1711, 'pulls on and puts off everything she wears twenty times before she resolves on it'. An elderly gallant with gout wrote to the *Spectator* in the same year describing the agony of going out to dinner in high-heeled shoes with a glazed wax-leather instep – a kindly person forcibly removed the shoes and replaced them with something soft. The same journal has a rare description of a Georgian gentleman without his finery: 'He was puffing along in the fields near Chelsea in his open waistcoat, a boy of fourteen in a livery carrying after him his cloak, upper cloak, hat, wig and sword. The poor lad was ready to sink with the load.'

In the mid-eighteenth century, however, men could acceptably present the shape of their bodies in public. The new mode was sparked off by a sweeping craze for antiquity and especially for discoveries in Greece and Italy of classical statuary; the statues were admired for being apparently nature unmarked by fashion or imperfections. Thus men's waistcoats,

which had previously concealed the lower parts, rose until they only reached the hips. Fashion expert Diana de Marly puts it as follows, 'The breeches and the flies were disclosed and, given the admiration for classical limbs, breeches became tighter and ever tighter, moulding the thighs and making the sexual bulge an unavoidable presence. Masculinity at its most blatant was making a comeback.'[6]

This trim rural look, right for towns as well as country, demanded skin-colour for waistcoats and breeches, giving at a distance an impression of nakedness. 'Taste now required ladies not to blush,' writes Miss de Marly, 'but to admire the perfect sculpture of male limbs'.

In the prudery that followed the Regency, women's dresses were expected to be fully figure-concealing, but there were plenty of women of the better classes who were impelled by vanity and other thoughts to expose their shapes. Brisk comments might be drawn from those who served them. In the 1830s a footman

With the Stuart period of the sixteenth century came low necklines for women and exaggerated attire for men

confided in his diary that the immodest dress of certain guests at dinner shocked him. 'It is quite disgusting to a modist eye to see the way the young ladies dress to attract the notice of gentlemen. They are nearly naked to the waist, only a little bit of dress hanging on the shoulder, the breasts are quite exposed except a little bit coming up to hide the nipples . . .'[7]

Victorian propriety conquered in the end and for women and men it became important, if they belonged to moneyed circles, to look decorously clothed from minute to minute. Women of the nineteenth century found indeed that a main occupation during a house party was changing clothes. Breakfast demanded a costume of velvet or silk or perhaps a riding habit; before lunch these clothes were discarded for tweeds, suitable wear for joining the guns, at tea-time tweeds gave way to a tea gown; and then it was time to dress for dinner when maids brought forward satins to be worn with jewels.[8]

Various nineteenth-century skirts hid the shape of the lower half of a woman so well that until around 1850 even the protruding tip of a shoe could seem erotic. However, a girl with good legs was not without vanity to the point of never wishing them to be seen. One way of showing them was to put on men's clothes and appear at transvestite balls. That was the course taken early in the nineteenth century by Tsarina Elizabeth of Russia, daughter of Peter the Great. She personally organized a number of balls of this kind at her Winter Palace in St Petersburg: the gentlemen wore false breasts but the ladies did not wear false calves.[9]

Byron's friend Caroline Lamb liked to show her legs by appearing at parties as a page. She was dressed in this way at her so-called *auto-da-fé* at

Girls often wished their legs
could be seen. This one has
achieved it by pretending
to be a soldier in the Civil
War of the mid-seventeenth
century

Brocket Hall in 1812 when (no longer Bryon's friend) she made a bonfire of her letters from Byron. Back in the seventeenth century numerous women changed their shape by wearing men's clothes when they covertly joined their husbands in the Civil War, adequately aping the sex of the troops. Some women, who were not wives following their men, met with criticism, and in July 1643 Charles I issued a proclamation concerning licentiousness. 'Let no woman presume to Counterfeit her Sex by wearing man's apparel under pain of the Severest punishment which law and our displeasure shall inflict.'[10] It was not effective.

One way for a vain Victorian girl to reveal a pretty leg was to be pushed by a young man on a swing, thus allowing a disarrangement of the skirt and perhaps even a Hogarthian romp. Modest girls did not wear underpants because these were considered male garments, and so swings provided a popular diversion in the eighteenth and nineteenth centuries.

Even the esteemed clergyman Francis Kilvert writes with zest in his diary of a wedding party which turned into a romp with 'the girls squealing and being tickled, not against their will'. He himself once had a private 'screaming romp with a young lady who in rolling about upset the candle and burst into peals of inextinguishable laughter'.

The arrival of the often charming hoop skirt around 1820 lessened slightly the mystery about girls' legs, for this type of stiffened crinoline floated lightly around the body and would sometimes tilt upwards revealingly even during a game of croquet. It was an item in the wardrobe of every properly vain young woman, and it offered material for satirical prints. Lovers and contraband could be shown hidden underneath. In one jocular drawing the hoop skirt is seen as both parachute and camper's tent. In real life the floating hoop skirt was potentially dangerous: Mrs Canter Cremers has written of the fire at the Maria Feast in Santiago Cathedral where the edge of a hoop skirt caught alight from a candle, causing a catastrophe.[11]

Although a man may be as vain as any woman, his body lends itself less well to reshaping. Nevertheless men did take to corsets for their middles from the

George IV at Brighton in the early nineteenth century. No corset could disguise his corpulence

11

eighteenth century onwards and they added padding to their shoulders and legs. George IV is renowned for finding that the firmest corset would not disguise his corpulence.

False calves were ordinary articles of commerce in the days before trousers, and were in men's wardrobes from the late eighteenth century and through much of the nineteenth. A demand for them increased when coats became shorter and tall leather boots were no longer worn: there was self-consciousness about the true shape of legs.

However, the artificial calves, needing three pairs of stockings for a natural effect, could bring embarrassment. Eline Canter Cremers gives an account of an army sergeant accorded a meeting in bed with a lady: he could not enjoy his situation at first for worry about what to do with his calves and three pairs of stockings, but he contrived to push them all uncomfortably beneath his pillow.[9]

Disguise of one sort or another is at the heart of vanity and part of the reason for the late nineteenth-century bustle, reaching out from behind with some sort of train, was to suggest that no lady possessed an actual posterior. The fact that women went mountaineering in their bustles is even stranger than that in the 1890s they took to cycling in skirts which touched the ground. It was years before easier and more practical clothes were accepted, but meanwhile the 1870s had seen a decline in the popularity of the crinoline. The appeal of this garment had spread to all classes and it had been worn by peasant girls in the fields, by maidservants and factory workers.

Edwardian times were good times for the rich and the vain. As Virginia Cowles has said in *Edward VII and his Circle*, 'more money was spent on clothes and more infidelities committed than ever before'. In the period of economic crisis affecting many after the 1914–18 war, the rich still liked to show themselves off in Swiss skiing resorts, in Paris and on the French Riviera.

But until the end of the Second World War clothes came to be governed less by vanity than restrained fashion and the occupation of the wearer. Then at the end of the 1940s vanity reasserted itself, especially on the part of men, the better-off men admiring their reflections in clothes of the New Edwardian style. Their type of suit was echoed in the 1950s by Teddy Boy dress. However, it should be said that the choice of these young men of drainpipe trousers and vulgarized drape jackets was largely motivated by a proper

Advertisement by Skinner and Co. of 1870 for bustles, or tournures, which exaggerated the contour of the behind. Some women went mountaineering in them

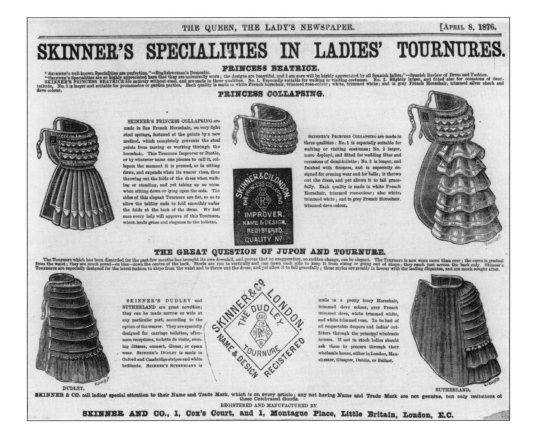

13

urge for self-assertion; they succeeded in this; the unlikely appearance of the Teddy Boys drew attention from the Press. They came on the scene with great speed, at the same time as American greasers and rockers in leather jackets.

There was nothing necessarily vain about women arranging to have an entirely flat stomach in the 1940s and '50s; nearly everyone had them and women took on girdles, elastic roll-ons and all-in-one corsets. In the same way, because it was expected of them, they chose garments so much like their husbands' as to be inter-changeable – duffle coats, sweaters, scarves and gloves.

How vain is a man who wears flowery ties? Possibly hardly at all. He may be advertising some-thing, such as his business. In the 1960s Patrick Lichfield began to wear frilled shirts and told a news-paper he owned twenty-six suits: he was establishing the fact that he was in business as a fashion photogra-pher. The young men of the sixties and seventies were surely vain, however, when they grew their hair to below the shoulders; only with a strong face was the mode acceptable. But fashion has always met and excused vanity.

Collective vanity was certainly apparent in the way the rock and roll garments were taken up, these stem-ming from the 1954 film *Rock Around the Clock* – the flower-printed shirts, the tight jeans and casual sweaters contrasting with the girls' full skirts over several petticoats. But what about the girls who took to the mini-skirt, launched in the 1960s, 'a garment so small that bottoms were visible', as Joan Nunn, histo-rian of fashion, has written? Such girls were happy to put aside the sophisticated look and take on the sweater-girl look in order to become childlike crea-tures from anywhere.

It seems that self-respect ends and vanity begins where there is an element of narcissism, where a person keeps checking with pleasure on his appearance. Punk styles of the late 1970s were those of bright rebels and they involved a deliberately anarchic and badly assorted assembly of garments wearable by both sexes. Here indeed a mockery was made of traditional vanity: hair would be dyed green or pink or orange and with egg white made to stand out in spikes from the head; safety pins were used not only for joining up clothes but also as piercing decorations for ear and nose and men wore one or more ear-rings. The ugliness of punk bands became notorious for their power to shock.

Cotton jeans, arriving in the early 1960s, are such a usual trousering for every social class and for both sexes that a visitor from afar would suppose them exempt from thoughts of vanity. Far from it; the fashion-conscious person has long wanted them soft, faded and distressed to the point of having tears. People have been found stone-washing their jeans, rubbing them with pumice stone or rinsing them out in the sea. Factories got in on the act early and one factory noted that twenty-five per cent of its manufacturing cost went on 'ageing'. It has been possible to buy from the United States second-hand jeans torn across the seat by the previous owner; the cost of such spoiled jeans being as much as brand-new 'designer' jeans.

In contrast to the trend among the young for extremes of informal clothing there was the emergence in the early 1980s, of the Sloane Ranger, Sloane being a reference to London's Sloane Square. This involved extra-correct dress and speech and always green Wellington boots for country wear. There was no rebellious element – boys and girls tried to look just like their parents. Jennifer Sharp of *Harpers and Queen* wrote in 1991: 'True Sloanes are like labradors – good-natured, good-looking, well-bred and friendly. The passing of time has allowed us to feel more affection for the Sloane Ranger.' (At the time of going to press the Sloane Rangers appear no longer to exist in their original form.)

Fashion, which has excused so much vanity, only just excused the stiletto heel of the 1960s thought to give a shapely leg; not only were feet damaged but also tiles, carpets, lawns and the floors of aircraft. The awkwardly high heels were effectively challenged by lower heels in the early 1980s.

It is age-old tradition rather than fashion which excuses the vanity of tattooing the body with permanent-blue designs and words. Tattooists are as busy today as in the past: their craft was practised among the ancient Britons whose woad was made tenacious by the pricking-in process. It is not only working-class boys who want to indelibly celebrate a friend, a notion or a design: young women of all classes are frequently tattooed, even if the work is rarely seen. An explanation for decoration of this sort – quite painful in the execution – could only emerge from an enquiry with masses of people being interviewed.

Fit young men with proper vanity took to the swimming-trunks style of the late 1970s, this consisting of little more than a pouch at the front and a triangle of cloth at the back. Anyone seeing them on a hot day could well conclude that clothes are superfluous and that the best form of vanity is to wear no clothes. But this implies a nice-looking body and exercised muscles.

2

A Large Bosom or a Small

The American is happy to bring his wife to the surgeon, thinking that she will regain all her beauty. It is with joy and insistence that he encourages her to have an operation. He often asks to be present in order to lavish encouragement on her and to discuss with me the best location for operating. The Englishman shares this point of view but is rarely present at the operation . . . In the northern countries the most complete masculine indifference prevails.

Dr Suzanne Noël, celebrated French
cosmetic surgeon, 1926.

Most cosmetic surgery in England is done by general surgeons as a part-occupation. Yet some may carry out in the course of a year 100 face lifts, 150 nose alterations and 50 operations on breasts – so it is suggested by London's Harley Medical Group.

Cosmetic surgery grows more sought after and twenty per cent of applicants are men. Some submit to it to keep a spouse or because they are in the public eye; but vanity in its most commonly accepted sense is the usual spur. For a woman (and equally for a man) the trauma of just getting older can prompt action; cosmetic surgery seems the means to a fresh start. It can, in a way, put the clock back. But in due course nature will take over and a return trip to the cosmetic surgeon will be necessary.

People have been having facial operations since civilizations began. Noses, for example, were being restored and repaired in India thousands of years ago. The Roman doctor Cornelius Celsus drew on Indian experience for his work and for his book *De Medicina* of AD 30, in which he wrote about plastic surgery for noses, lips and ears (the first writings about such operations in surgical literature). It must be said, though, that these operations were to deal with injuries and gross defects of nature and not just to concoct good looks. Terrors, needless to say, were involved for the patients.

Modern cosmetic surgery dates from around 1885 when various local anaesthetics were invented as improvements on laughing gas. In 1887 the surgeon John Roe of Rochester, New York, published an essay called 'The Deformity Termed Pug Nose', which described treatment. The first abdominal operation for overweight was performed by Howard Kelly of Baltimore in 1889. He relieved a man of 15 lb of fat. The first face lift was carried out by Eugene Hollander of Berlin in 1901, for a Polish aristocrat who offered detailed sketches of what he wanted done. An actress underwent this operation in 1906 at the hands of Erich Lexer, a German, who was talented as a sculptor and painter as well as a surgeon.

Results in those days looked tight, mask-like and only good in parts. Photographs survive. Hollander believed it was necessary for a patient to feel very uncomfortable tension for up to three days. Robert Gersumy of Vienna thought he had the answer to the tight look: injecting paraffin wax instead of any scalpel work. But he did harm to the reputation of cosmetic surgery after writing enthusiastically about this in 1903. The injections did indeed remove wrinkles, but only for a short time; they caused much discomfort and before long the cosmetic results were dreadful.[1]

Such well-known doctors as Joseph Safian of New York recall patients begging them in the 1920s to deal with the effects of paraffin injected into the face. Hundreds of cosmetic surgeons struggled almost hopelessly to remove masses of facial tissue infiltrated by solidified paraffin wax: the whole permeated part had to be taken away. Indeed, work on paraffinomas, as they were called, constituted a major part of the early cosmetic surgeon's practice.

A large number of the cosmetic operations in the early twentieth century seem to have been performed by people stigmatized by the medical profession as charlatans, often because they advertised incautiously. And certainly there was some irresponsible advertising in the Press. The Princess Bust Developer was said to do wonders and a certain Bust Cream and Food was unrivalled for developing not only the bust but also the neck and arms.

Bust developers, abdominal supports, chin straps and wrinkle removers were manufactured mainly in Chicago, America's centre for folk songs, folk nostrums and folk medicines. It was in Chicago that Dr Charles Conrad Miller, graduate of Louisville College of Medicine, wisely opened a cosmetic surgery in 1903. Soon the public flocked to it, partly because of the many articles he wrote – such is the power of the printed word. Dr Miller, only partly a quack, wrote a book called *Cosmetic Surgery* which caused a stir in 1907 and is still looked at by surgeons.

When a woman consults the family physician regarding a defect of facial outline the family physician is likely to laugh. But cosmetic surgery is a special field worthy of the closest study by the ablest of our profession, for he who operates has at stake the future happiness of the patient. Operations for improving the appearance cannot be botched. The criminal carelessness of advertisers is unbelievable to those who have not seen the results . . . Many who have consulted me have been mutilated . . .

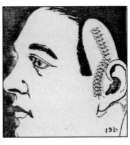

The most extensive face-lift shown in Dr Miller's book of 1925. The incision was closed by tension buttons

Dr Miller described the excision of crow's feet lines, the correction of thick or inverted lips, nose improvement, changing the size of the mouth, removal of facial lines, making prominent ears lie flat and the obliteration of tattoos. He pioneered treatment for bag-like folds of skin around the eyes, issuing photographs of this work which influenced surgical practice. He described the creation for a young girl of a dimple, 'located by her smile', remarking that he had to be 'forced into the performance of this particular operation'.

Dr Miller did his operations under the local anaesthesia of a weak cocaine solution – half a grain in an ounce of boiled water. He used gentle techniques. He sewed with fine cambric needles and to avoid tiny marks never tied his stitches too tight.[2]

With the pace and glamour that marked the 1920s, bright predictions for the future of cosmetic surgery came true, and even more patients arrived at Dr Miller's new clinic in a fashionable part of Chicago. Having there the assistance of four nurses, he performed cosmetic procedures one after another, sending patients wanting a general anaesthetic to a nearby hospital.

Dr Miller's prose style drew attention from many outside the medical world and no less a writer than S.J. Perelman wrote of him as follows under the heading 'Mid-Winter Facial Trends':

> The doctor starts off casually enough with instructions for correcting outstanding ears, which range all the way from tying them flat to the head to some pretty violent surgery. Personally, I have found that a short length of three-quarter-inch manila hemp bound stoutly about the head, the knot protruding just below one's hat, adds a rakish twist to the features and effectively prisons ears inclined to flap in the wind . . .[3]

Other surgeons often disagreed with Miller, only to take up his inventions as their own years later. It is a fact, though, that his long career was marred by some of his experiments. In 1926 he wrote of curious materials implanted through a tube to correct depressions and lines, these including, in his words, 'bits of braided silk, bits of silk floss, particles of celluloid, vegetable ivory and several other foreign materials'.

With the depression of the early 1930s, demand for cosmetic surgery was reduced and Dr Miller became busy with general surgery. He wrote modestly: 'As one grows older one finds more satisfaction in doing operations which cure disease rather than those which merely satisfy vanity.' For all that, cosmetic surgery remained his great interest and in the words of Dr B.O. Rogers, his book '*Cosmetic Surgery* justifies our regarding him as the father of modern cosmetic surgery'.[4]

Dr Miller issued forty-four papers as well as the book, and surgeons prepared to do cosmetic work on his better principles became active after the First World War, in which wonders were done restoring wounded men. Further, many face-lifting and other beautifying operations were undertaken on civilians in the period 1918–30.

Raymond Passot wrote in 1919 of the great social value of cosmetic operations, their stimulating effect on morale, urging that women should not leave things until the skin had collapsed. In 1920 Adulbert Bettman was encouraging face-lift patients by assuring them that little discomfort was involved. 'One woman,' he writes, 'after having the operation, proceeded immediately to a local department store where she bought a hat suitable for her now youthful appearance.' Jacques Joseph of Berlin was genuinely concerned about the poor and the oppressed, and in 1921 gave accounts of wrinkle-removal to help prematurely-aged working women of forty-five to get employment.

There was in the twenties an unexplained fashion for a flat chest – see any contemporary photograph or drawing – and some women found their efforts at strapping down to be inadequate. Women with heavy breasts went to a surgeon in despair: their trouble, they said, was too much to live with. The surgeon was able to effect with difficulty a reduction. Then, within a few years, came a fashion-reversal from America. And bosom culture was mandatory.

Up and down the country English women were now buying special brassières and trying to stimulate reduced breasts to fill them. Some gave up and bought inflatable busts with a short tube for topping up. Others, preferring the real thing, returned to their surgeons for an expensive surgical enlargement.

For the women of Japan an awkwardness arose after 1945 when fashion called for the wearing of bust-conscious Western clothes made for Western figures: Japanese women are flat-chested by nature, a circumstance catered for by the kimono. Cosmetic-surgery clinics began to multiply in Tokyo for the implanting of tissues and bags. The clinics were visited, too, by Japanese men, proving unexpectedly vain about their eyes, noses and ears.[5]

In England nose operations took off. Rhinoplasty soon became a refined art and today surgeons can shorten, lengthen, tilt or straighten exactly as wished. They say the hardest part of the job can be to convince a patient that it may not be the nose which is at fault but the chin, which could need adding to with a slice of silicone; once the face is so augmented, a person's existing nose may look right. A surgeon writes: 'The nose is a peninsula, not an island. It makes no sense

Hats and dresses of the period just before the First World War. Breasts, it will be noted, are already beginning to disappear

unless considered in relation to the mainland, the face.'

The brilliant demonstration of what cosmetic surgery could do for the wounded of the Second World War has led to an ever increasing demand for facial improvement. Because of the derogatory sense of the word vanity, cosmetic surgeons are anxious to tell prospective patients that they are not being just vain in wanting a change in their appearance. The directors of the Harley Medical Group in London, providing all kinds of cosmetic surgery, are conscious of an unadventurous attitude on the part of general practitioners. 'Prospective patients seeking their advice,' they write in the brochure, 'are likely to meet attitudes dismissing the benefits of treatment as simply vanity. But the medical profession is gradually becoming more aware of the psychological benefits to be gained from self improvement.' Even the best plastic surgeons were formerly magisterial about beautifying work. Now they increasingly exchange views and attend seminars all over the world on how best to correct and improve on nature.

People with certain facial defects are indeed fortunate today. At the beginning of the twentieth century, apallingly, little girls might be made to wear the equivalent of tight corsets on their faces. Edith Sitwell, the distinguished poet, underwent torture because of her parents' efforts to make her prettier. A surgeon put her into nose slams; but the treatment was ineffective. Osbert Sitwell relates in his autobiography: 'Her nose was still not the shape for which my father had bargained, so the reign of iron and manacles began. The harm inflicted on her nervous system and her physique proved to be costly, though not irreparable; it took months to break down the adhesions that had formed . . .'

Television performer Marylyn Davies recovering from the removal of a bump on her nose, 1959

Every third advertisement on American television is for plastic surgery, according to Lisa Armstrong in the *Independent on Sunday Magazine*, 1991. In 1989 Ivana Trump appeared on television after having such an operation. 'What have you done to yourself?' asked the interviewer. 'You look *wonderful*.' Mrs Trump indulged in understatement. 'I just changed my make-up and played with my hair a bit.' She did not say that to stave off the depredations affecting a lady of 41 she had undergone extensive and by no means fail-safe surgery; the work took in her lips, cheeks, breasts, thighs, stomach and bottom.

In parts of America, according to the magazine *Blitz*, the sixteen-year-olds of 1991 no longer asked for a car for their birthday, they asked for cosmetic surgery – a request mildly insulting to the couple who gave them birth. The search for physical perfection is at its most urgent in Los Angeles where the display of bodies on the beach inspires a restless pumping-up of figures and faces. Muscle implants are popular. For those not happy with their calves the answer is of course a silicone implant. As for hair transplants, Americans need only flick through the advertisements in *LA Weekly* to hit upon somewhere to go.

Those who may be called the ambassadors of cosmetic surgery, as Mrs Trump may be, are on full view as performers at the time of writing: Brigitte Nielson and Dolly Parton with their enlarged bosoms, Michael Jackson with his changed skin colour, Cher with a type of perfection produced by all possible treatments, the pop star Madonna who had her lips injected with collagen to fill them out, Jane Fonda who admits that the excellence of her form was the result of silicone injections and Kirk Douglas with his pleasing but slightly overstretched face lift. The list is endless.

3

Speech Without Laughter

Why do people agree to give after-dinner speeches? According to Julian Critchley the answer can only be vanity, 'a quality,' he says, 'which is shared in almost equal proportions by actors, parsons and politicians. There is pleasure to be had from the sound of one's own voice'.[1]

In first century Rome the schools of rhetoric were criticized for encouraging the vanity of speaking in public. 'They make idiots of our young men,' wrote Petronius, '. . . the manner of speech demanded is a ludicrous amalgamation of honeyed words and delicate phrases.' In present-day Italy a person's natural vanity in whatever capacity is flattered at all times to render life decorous and agreeable, to make the wariest feel more confident and agreeable.

There is a mode of address so common in Italy 'one breathes it,' writes Luigi Barzini in *The Italians*, 'like the violets in the spring, without exactly recognizing what it is that gives one such a delicate sensation'. Everybody is constantly being vaguely praised by everybody else.

A decrepit man is always told he looks years younger; an old hag that she is more beautiful this year than last, today than yesterday, tonight than this morning. There is almost imperceptible flattery in the obsequiousness with which your advice is sought in matters in which you have no particular experience. Then there is the use of academic or other titles; people affix them to your name, as if to prove that you so visibly deserve such honours that it is impossible you have not been awarded them.

A middle-class man is called *dottore* in his youth and becomes *commendatore* when over forty. Ordinary letters are addressed to the 'most egregious', 'illustrious', 'celebrated', 'eminent', 'renowned' Signore. Tailors praise your build. Dentists exclaim: 'You have the teeth of an ancient Roman!' The doctor cannot help remarking that he has rarely encountered an influenza as baffling as yours.

Because of the innate vanity of the Italians, Dr Barzini writes, transparent deceptions are constantly employed 'to give a man the most precious of all Italian feelings, that of being a distinct personality deserving special consideration'. To pay the full price for a theatrical performance is equivalent to admitting that one is nobody and has no friends.[2]

How much more pleasant is all this consideration for people's feelings than vain rigidity and finding fault. In eighteenth-century England a person was not even allowed to laugh and Lord Chesterfield writes in *Letters to his Son*, 1743. 'I must particularly warn you against laughing: I could heartily wish that you may often be seen to smile, but never heard to laugh while you live . . . In my mind there is nothing so illiberal, and so ill-bred, as audible laughter . . . nobody has ever heard me laugh.'

In truth, the rules about never laughing probaby arose from concern about bad teeth, missing teeth and the occasional crude, unsteady replacement. Lord Chesterfield lost all his teeth when quite young 'through inattention', and certainly would have wished to avoid what he called 'the shocking distortion of the face' occasioned by laughing.

The taboo was not new; Erasmus in the sixteenth century advised against laughing. During the dialogue of Swift's *Polite Conversation*, 1738, a woman who laughs draws this rebuke from the man beside her: 'You can't laugh but you must show your teeth.' He meant that it might have been all right had that not been necessary. Swift himself, according to Dr Johnson, 'stubbornly resisted any tendency to laughter'. And Pope never showed the inside of his mouth – 'By no merriment either of others or of his own,' said Johnson, 'was he ever excited to laughter.'

The rule that laughing was to be avoided as silly and disagreeable (though just permissible for a woman if she held up a fan) faded out at the end of the nineteenth century when improvements in dentistry began to be enjoyed by people of means. And Hilaire Belloc could write early in the twentieth century:

Jonathan Swift, who resisted laughing, at the age of forty-two. A portrait in the manner of C. Jervas, 1709

> There's nothing worth the wear of winning
> But laughter and the love of friends.

Avoid speaking of yourself ('if it be at all possible') was anther rule put forward by Lord Chesterfield to his son in the eighteenth century: 'Such is the natural pride and vanity of our hearts, that it perpetually breaks out. Some abruptly speak advantageously of themselves, without either pretence or provocation. Others proceed more artfully.' He warns his son against pleasing his vanity by dwelling on the reflec-

tion of others and seeking to profit by reflected glory. Some people are so vain, he says, as to put forward in conversation 'little extraneous objects which have not the least relation to themselves, such as being descended from, related to or acquainted with people of distinguished merit. Have they themselves more merit from these accidents? Certainly not . . . a rich man never borrows.'

Vanity can cause a person to be boring, insistent and unwilling to admit that the remarks of others may be more interesting than his; and such symptoms of vanity were observed by Theophrastus 2,300 years ago. 'The vain and garrulous man will sit beside someone whom he does not know and begin to praise his own wife, or tell a story of a dream he had the night before. As he warms to his business, he will remark that the younger generation have not the manners of the old . . .'

A vain bore, wrote Horace in about 35 BC, forgets the point or concentration of his narrative. He indulges in unnecessary precision, wishing to fix names and dates that have little bearing on his discourse. 'It must,' he will say, 'have been in October – no, it can't have been, because we were in Copenhagen then – no it may have been in early November – anyway, it doesn't matter, and to cut a long story short . . .'

The vain and boring woman of the 1750s, clustered about with servants and a docile husband, occasionally had cruel ways of making herself felt. In a Georgian handbook by Jane Collier, *The Art of Tormenting*, such a woman is ironically given this tip for use when her respectable paid-companion looks provoked. She is told to say to her: 'I beseech you, Child, to spare your frowns for those that will fear them; and keep your disdainful looks for the footmen, when they make

Alexander Pope, aged forty-nine, who never showed the inside of his mouth.

love to you; which by your flirting airs, I make no doubt they are encouraged to do . . .'

Richmal Crompton's vain woman of 1928, deciding at a tea party that not enough fuss is being made of her, has a few words ready:

> She rose and said with an air of great dignity: 'Mrs Hawkins, I am suffering from a headache. May I go into your drawing-room and lie down?' She had often found this focused the attention of everyone upon her. It did in this instance. They all leapt to their feet solicitously, fussed about her, escorted her to the drawing-room, drew down the blinds and left her well pleased with the stir she had made.[3]

Her author was also pleased, the removal to another room being essential to the plot of her story.

For centuries the higher social classes of England have been so vain as to invent little rules about utterance to demonstrate their difference: outside the family they are not referred to. To this day there is a ban on such perfectly good words as toilet, dentures, lounge, horse-riding and greens. The whole list is quite long, but not so long as formerly in Germany, where an acquaintance of aristocratic birth said he had been punched in the head by his mother for saying 'angenehm', a word widely used to signify 'pleased to meet you', but considered by some to be too 'common' for use.

In the thirteenth century, Chaucer's prioress, or Madame Eglentine, shows her would-be elevated social position by her singing in church, 'entuned in hir nose ful semely', and by her way of breaking into French, which 'she spak ful faire and fetishly'.[4] It was long an upper class vanity to lard conversations with as many French snippets as possible. Queen Victoria decorated all her letters in this way, describing someone's house, for example, as *'un vrai bijou'*.

The table manners of the socially aspiring Madame Eglentine matched her elocution. 'She leet no morsel from her lippes fall ne wette hir fingers in hir sauce depe.' Nevertheless so pleasant was she that her ruder companions on the pilgrimage to Canterbury seem never to have called her stuck-up. If she had appeared a few hundred years later at Versailles she would have been reproved by Louis XIV for pretentious vanity. Despite the civilized splendours of his palace, the king could not stand finicky eating and restraint over using the fingers. According to Sir Harold Nicolson, he was so much irritated by the clean feeding habits of Mme de Thianges, who always used a fork, that he told his valet to put hairs into her plate.[5]

How the vainer members of the non-laughing upper classes sounded centuries ago is largely guesswork: most had regional accents and they were loyally vain about them. But a few facts are known. In the sixteenth century a vain woman of fashion turned a short 'o' into an 'a', saying 'a pax on it' for 'a pox on it'. In the late seventeenth century Vanbrugh, in his play *The Relapse or Virtue in Danger*, tries to show by means of spelling the sounds for his metropolitan character Lord Foppington. There is 'naw' for 'now', 'sprauts' for 'sprouts', 'raund' for 'round' and 'resalve' for 'resolve'. (At this time, under Italian influence, changes were taking place in the French language and *'François'* became *'Français'*.)

In eighteenth-century England the foppish took to saying 'obleeged' for 'obliged' and 'goold' for 'gold'. Dr Johnson most reasonably pronounced 'great' to rhyme with 'heat' and 'meat', but was criticized by

Lord Chesterfield who had himself adopted, 150 years too soon, the current pronunciation of 'grate'.

In his book of 1791, *The Critical Pronouncing Dictionary*, J. Walker tries to indicate proper usage for the upper-class person. Only one of his recommended pronunciations makes sense today: 'huntin' and 'fishin'' as used by the Edwardian set early in the twentieth century. His advised pronunciation of the words 'either' and 'neither' to rhyme with 'breather' is the opposite of that now in normal use. He thought that to say 'feller' for 'fellow' was 'almost too despicable for notice'. Yet 'feller' is often heard today.

During the early 1960s the top-drawer pronunciation of 'have' became 'hev'. It was widely heard and the observant novelist Norman Collins said he believed a new pronunciation had come to stay. In the event it lasted a short time only, becoming obsolete like the long-running pronunciation of 'cross' and 'off' as 'crorse' and 'orf'.

In the early 1940s the list of words for the decently vain to avoid was different, though not perhaps shorter, than today. Here is Nancy Mitford's character Uncle Matthew discussing Fanny with her aunt in *The Pursuit of Love*:

> I hope Fanny's school is doing her all the good you think it is. She picks up some dreadful expressions there. I hear poor Fanny asking for notepaper. What is this education? Fanny talks about mirrors and mantelpieces, handbags and perfume. She *takes* sugar in her coffee and I have no doubt that if she is ever fortunate enough to catch a husband she will call his father and mother Father and Mother . . . Fancy hearing one's wife talk about notepaper – the irritation. [The aunt now turns to Fanny] Fanny

darling, it is called writing-paper you know – don't let us hear any more about note, please.

Such vanities of speech belonged of course to the upper classes only and are the result of moving in the same circles and going to the same schools and wishing to seem a little superior. It is only arguably right to use the word vanity.[6]

There are also words in popular use known as genteelisms, whose utterance may or may not denote a foppish speaker. These are thought less plebeian, less vulgar or less improper than the words which would come naturally: thus visitors are asked to step in, not come in; children go to college, not school; people pass away instead of die; enough becomes sufficient, smells become odours and sweat perspiration.

In his *Modern English Usage* of 1926 H.W. Fowler lists forty-two genteelisms of which about half are still recognizable. The disparaging word genteel has itself radically changed its meaning over the centuries. Throughout the eighteenth century it meant well-bred and, according to Henry James's *English Hours* of 1905, it was still being used in that sense at the start of the twentieth century.

Any discussion of vanity of speech is doomed to descend to a discussion of class-conscious words and to the snobbery of 'U' and 'Non U' speech as written about by Nancy Mitford. This chapter has already so descended. The fact seems to be that there is no phrase in English which necessarily denotes vanity and that the most pompous remark can be uttered acceptably if it is in context, if it suits the company or if it is some sort of joke.

4

The Insolence of the Dandy

The dandy is vain and arrogant by definition and among ordinary people the word has always been acceptable as a term of abuse. In Thackeray's *Vanity Fair*, 1848, Becky describes George Osborne as 'that selfish humbug, that low-bred Cockney dandy who had neither wit nor manners nor heart'.

The true dandies of two hundred years ago considered they were both above the common herd and above criticism. 'Do you think I could ever wear a watch?' asks the dandy hero of Bulwer-Lytton's novel *Pelham*, 1828. 'I know nothing more plebeian; what can anyone but a man of business who has nine hours for his counting house and one for his dinner, ever possibly want to know the time for?'

Dandies began to blossom in the late eighteenth century when plenty of men were both unemployed and well-off; such men were thankful their country had avoided the nominal class equality produced over the Channel by the French Revolution. The name, accepted by all, is thought to have come from the 1770s' American song 'Yankee doodle dandy'. Many of the fashionable young dandies had visited Italy and brushed against Italian culture; they called themselves macaronis as a swipe against their elders who belonged to the Beefsteak Club and they became

A macaroni ready for a party, from a contemporary print of 1782

notorious for wild parties and affected behaviour.

They wore make-up, tall wigs – even three feet high and capped with a tiny tricorn – striped breeches, waistcoats, short flared coats and a nosegay. The idea was to exaggerate the dress of the day. A print shows a stout country squire horrified at recognizing his son got up in full macaroni attire.

Macaronis thought themselves arbiters of taste and fashion while others thought them fatuous. 'You are a macaroni, Sir, you cannot ride,' Boswell told Dr Johnson, to prod him into activity on their highland journey.[1]

All dandies were influenced by the exceptionally vain Beau Brummell, an old Etonian with inherited money who was patronized for a time by the Prince Regent. He bathed three times a day, actually wore clean linen and made the ritual of his morning toilet legendary. This lasted over two hours and the tying of his starched cravat became a sight watched by the prince. However, most of the showy dandies with their pinched waists, bulging breasts and raised epaulettes were in fact copying only in part the style of Brummell whose concern was to be elaborately inconspicuous rather than flamboyant.

The dandies may have been clean but their bearing was arrogant – vain in the worst sense. 'The highest triumph of the English dandy,' wrote Prince Pückler-Muskau, 'is to appear with wooden manners and to contrive even his civilities so that they are as near as may be to affronts . . . to treat his best friends as if he did not know them, to cut them . . .'[2]

Cutting was one of Brummell's specialities, according to Dorothy M. George. The procedure is illustrated in a set of three plates of 1827 after M. Egerton: the 'Cut Celestial', the 'Cut Infernal' and the 'Cut Direct'.

Beau Brummell aged twenty-seven, in 1805. He made the ritual of his morning toilet legendary, and the Prince Regent sometimes watched him tying his starched cravat

In one print a dandy walking in London meets an acquaintance, perhaps his tailor, and stares first at the sky and then at the ground – an exercise needing no more than cheek. In popular prints there were two types of dandy: the typical kind, absurd and languid, and the would-be dandy, imitating in a squalid room the admired manners and catch phrases. Simple foppery, or affectation, in men's dress had been around harmlessly for centuries, but full dandyism as it flourished in the Regency had repercussions for a limited time in the world of ideas and politics. The monarchy admired a dandy and so, to an extent, did the aristocracy.

He was a creature perfect in externals and careless of anything below the surface; he stood for superiority, irresponsibility and inactivity. That dandyism could in fact be more than a frivolous preoccupation is shown by a book on the subject containing 370 pages which was published in 1960: Ellen Moers' scholarly work *The Dandy, Brummell to Beerbohm*.

Novels were written about the Regency dandies. The most influential work was Bulwer-Lytton's *Pelham or the Adventures of a Gentleman*, 1828, which charted the course of a dandy who grew out of frivolity and insolence to become a useful politician. The book was a covert attack on dandyism by a man who had himself been a dandy.

Pelham is a classic example in his impudence, affectation and self-love, and much of the novel shows him absorbed in the biggest of dandy concerns, matters of dress. Rules for male attire are seen to go from the principles of colour to the minutiae of coat tails, collars, rings and shoe strings. Pelham, fully dressed and scented, is described complaining about his looking glass to a woman he is staying with. 'Good Heavens! what an unbecoming glass it is! placed just opposite to me, too! Could it not be removed while I stay here? Oh! by the by, Lady Roseville, do you patronize Bohemian glasses? For my part, I have one which I only look at when I am out of humour; it throws such a lovely flush upon the complexion, that it revives my spirits for the rest of the day.'

Pelham has the ultra-vain man's scorn for people

others accept as correct, such as country gentlemen. 'Shooting is a most barbarous amusement only fit for majors in the army and royal dukes . . . the mere walking is bad enough.' He describes the working classes, whom he rarely meets, as 'the unknown vulgar'. He is careful of his comfort to the point of delicacy, and ventures reluctantly into a strange house or country inn in fear of the shock that refined senses may suffer from uncouth surroundings. More than once he has been introduced to 'a comfortless sort of dressing-room, without a fireplace, where I found a yellow-ware jug and basin and a towel of so coarse a huckaback that I did not dare adventure its rough texture next my complextion'.

Invited to dine with an epicure, Pelham takes with him a bundle of specially designed cutlery – a shallow spoon, a tiny fork and a blunt knife – to 'guard against my weakness of eating with too great rapidity'.

Dandies, standing for superiority, irresponsibility and inactivity. A print by Richard Dighton of 1818

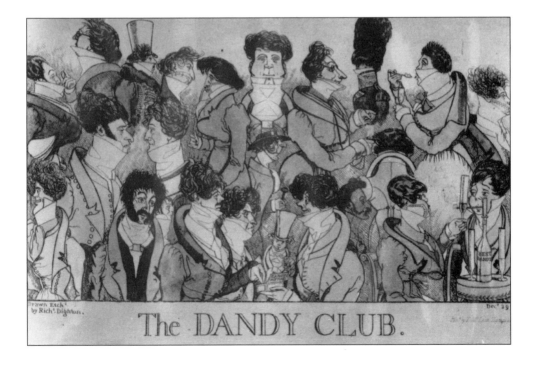

'It is a most unhappy failing,' he says, 'for one often hurries over in one minute what ought to have afforded the fullest delight for a period of five.' Pelham goes beyond the limits set by Brummell for an aesthete and represents the more extreme dandy who was to appear at the end of the 1830s.

Dandies were noticed by Jane Austen – as was the fact that some of them never married. In *Sense and Sensibility*, 1798, Lucy remarks of a man: 'One never thinks of married men being beaux.' The dandy brotherhood took to wearing clothes that copied coachmen's clothes and Jane Austen wrote in *Northanger Abbey*, 1797, that a certain gentleman drove a curricle better than a coachman: 'His hat sat so well and the innumerable capes of his great coat looked so becomingly important.'

Benjamin Disraeli, later Lord Beaconsfield, was exuberantly a dandy and received attention thereby at the time when he was seeking to win a seat in Parliament in the 1830s. With his long black ringlets and handsome semitic features, he made a noticeable figure as he went about in a black velvet, satin-lined coat, purple trousers with a gold band down the seam, a figured scarlet waistcoat and lace ruffles covering the hands. But his eloquence as a speaker had nothing of the dandy about it and belied his languid appearance.[3]

Charles Dickens, the extolled and monumentally hardworking author, was a dandy, too: in youth especially, but also in his latter years as a lecturer in America when 'the vivid tints of Mr Dickens' drew criticism. The young Dickens liked to wear a swallow-tail coat with a high velvet collar, a billowing black satin stock, a crimson or green velvet waistcoat and very tight trousers.

Dandyism was quite out of fashion in the smoky industrial towns of the 1850s and male dress became

Benjamin Disraeli, later Lord
Beaconsfield, aged twenty-
nine. By or after Daniel
Maclise

black and presented deep and almost greasy folds;
dark straggly beards were worn by men over forty.
Yet among the blackness and the beards there was for
many years a dandyish vanity about station in life on
the part of those who were well off without having to
work: the fact that a great nation across the Channel
had become a republic, where all men were said to be
equal, made it necessary to insist on difference. In
books for children the lower orders were told to look

up to those of higher rank, God having ordained that some should be rich and some poor.[4]

People of dandyish type were written about in late nineteenth-century novels, but these were not proper Regency dandies. The word dandy has been loosely used with hindsight about people who lived after and well before the Regency. Harold Nicolson thought he had identified a Roman dandy in Martial's Cotilus: 'He curled his hair, he scented himself with cinnamon and balsam, he was an authority on who was related to whom, he loved gossiping with smart women and he would hum little snatches from Spanish and Egyptian tunes.'[5]

Fenja Gunn writes of people who could be called dandies at the court of James I. They were young men who lacked the qualities of the Elizabethan courtier whose virility they replaced with a feminine manner: the king's reputation encouraged effeminacy. 'The Jacobean dandy practised innumerable affectations with the aid of scent bottles, fans and perfumed gloves; and a single lock of hair was allowed to remain at shoulder length, tied with a silk ribbon'. This so-called love lock was still worn when Charles I came to the throne in 1625.[6] The question arises: was there something specific about all dandies' sexual orientation? On the evidence, it can be guessed that at least half were fully heterosexual.

Thackeray identified the Victorian child dandy. His example was Georgy aged eleven, grandson of George Osborne. The little boy had 'fancy trousers, fancy waistcoats and fancy jackets enough to furnish a school of little dandies. He had white waistcoats for evening parties and little cut velvet waistcoats for dinners'. Georgy dressed for dinner every day and without even trying he had picked up the insolence of the classic dandy. But his antics at the dinner table did not

Charles Dickens carefully posing in middle age

please Mr Osborne's friends as much as they pleased Mr Osborne. 'Colonel Fogey was not interested in seeing the little boy half tipsy. Mr Sergeant Toffy's lady felt no particular gratitude when, with a twist of his elbow, he tilted a glass of port wine over her yellow satin and laughed at the disaster . . .'[7]

Dandy-type, class-ridden insolence is rare now among adults. Here is an example from the 1930s given in the memoirs of a maidservant at Cliveden. At dinner one evening

a public figure was talking to Lady Astor as a footman was serving him. 'I need a skivvy for my kitchen. Can any of your servants recommend one?'

'What kind of servant do you want?'

'Oh, any little slut will do.'

The footman stepped back and went white, but the butler caught him just as he was about to pour some hot sauce over the guest's head.[8]

However, servants, too, often behaved with the snobbishness of dandies if they worked for grand families. Footmen wearing livery, perhaps richly trimmed with silver, and maidservants in gowns well adjusted to their shapes and in hats adorned with ribbons had no doubt that notice and respect was their due.

The most vain group must include actors and actresses, dandies indeed. They tend to be concerned at all times with their images, including when off duty at home. And because of their training and gifts they can readily appear to be someone different; they can act in real life. Sir Lawrence Olivier often assumed this or that role and his wife Joan Plowright said on television: 'I never know when he is acting and when he isn't – I can't quite tell. It's a bit eerie.'

5

Painted Ladies and Gentlemen

Cosmetics of a kind have been used for reasons of vanity and sexual attraction since the earliest days of recorded history: the anointing of kings with pleasant-smelling oils and unguents was a custom common among all ancient peoples.

Most information about cosmetics in the distant past has been collected from Egypt. When the Tutankhamen tomb was opened in 1922 vases and pots were still fragrant from the oils they had contained. A substance for darkening the eyes, long thought to be kohl, an antimony compound, was now found on analysis to be a mixture of lead sulphide, malachite, charcoal, lampblack and soot. The ingredients of an Egyptian wrinkle remover were oil, wax, incense and cypress berries.

A principal cosmetic of the ancient Greeks was scent. In a third-century BC treatise on plants, Theophrates was able to describe the parts of plants from which perfume materials could be extracted, and he noted that certain plants had fixative powers.

The Romans made little use of cosmetics – so it appears – until the Empire grew powerful. After the conquest of the Greeks, the Egyptians and other Eastern peoples, both men and women took to a variety of cosmetics: hair bleaches, eye shadow, scented

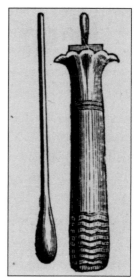

Ancient Egyptian make-up container and utensils.

body oils and face powder consisting of chalk and white lead. Teeth were even rubbed over with pumice. A fashionable Roman woman often had a slave, an ornatrix, who acted as a skilled cosmetician.

There is no information about the use of cosmetics for a long time after the fall of Rome, though soldiers and pilgrims returning from the Crusades are supposed to have acquainted Europeans with Eastern beauty practices. However, it seems certain that the English cover-up of body smells with fragrant oils and essences, which took the place of cleanliness, began in the fourteenth century – public baths of the Roman kind were widely forbidden by the Church, nudity being equated with lewdness.

As the *Michelin Guide* observes, in the thirteenth century there were twenty-six public baths in Paris. Under Louis XIV only two were left, the king remarking that he never had a bath. A bathtub remaining in his palace was thought to be superfluous and was removed to the gardens as part of a fountain. Earlier, Queen Elizabeth I had revealed that she bathed once a month, 'whether it was required or not'.

The face was all that was washed. Instead of body-washing there took place a liberal use of strong scent, and this went on till well into the nineteenth century. The eleventh Duke of Norfolk hated the sight of water, according to Osbert Sitwell, and tried to ignore its existence. But others washed him on occasion when he became helpless from drink.

At a sign from him that he was about to lose consciousness, a servant would ring the bell three times; when four footmen would immediately answer it, bearing a kind of stretcher. In absolute silence and with a dexterity that betrayed long practice, they lifted him on to it and with a gentle swinging motion removed his enormous bulk from the room. If he was quite insensible and unable to resist, they would sometimes take it upon themselves to remove his clothes and scrub his body with soap and water: a highly necessary rite . . .[1]

A popular Elizabethan skin clearer was largely oil of vitriol: to hide the scars of smallpox a thick application might be used of white lead, vinegar and sulphur, this producing a smooth whiteness which became eventually a ravaged, mummified mask; whitening the skin with mercury water and ceruse could lead to gastric trouble and the shakes.[2] Elizabethan women were prepared to work hard to achieve the pink, white and golden look which men liked. John Marston, the sixteenth-century poet and dramatist gave a detailed specification for the ideal English beauty:

The face should be round and ruddy, the forehead smooth, high and white, the eyebrows small delicate and marked with a pencil, the lips coral or like cherries, the eyes lamplike but downcast. The cheeks should show the rose and lily in combat and be dimpled like the chin, the neck, snow-white and round like an ivory pillar holding the head high, the ears round and compact, the hair a rich golden yellow.

The golden yellow hair, much desired by Latin ladies on the continent, was a goal achieved there only with much trouble. They would sit on their roofs, faces covered, hair spread out over wide-brimmed crownless hats so that the sun, damaging to the complexion, would help the work of whatever bleach they had applied to the head.

Although milk did not enjoy in the later Middle Ages the reputation it had in Roman times as a beauty bath, it was still thought good for the complexion. Tanning of the skin was a circumstance every Elizabethan took care to avoid. In addition to wearing hats and masks, the ladies used quantities of lemon water in which a handful of 'sublimate finely pow-

Queen Elizabeth I in middle life, reported to have had a bath once a month whether she needed it or not

dered' was dissolved to bleach away any trace of darkness. A red face was not acceptable even on men.

The sense of vanity was so strong in some people that they applied soliman, which perfectly got rid of such blemishes as spots and warts by removing the outer layer of skin, slightly consuming the layer of flesh underneath and causing a recession of the gums. Soliman was a sublimate of mercury and described, even in the sixteenth century, as biting in its action.

Men, almost as much as women, used cosmetics and were as vain about the cut and colour of a beard as about the cut and colour of doublet and hose. The Elizabethan period saw an enormous increase in the use of perfumes. Every grand house had a still room where aromatic waters and remedies were made from recipes kept and handed down from generation to generation.

The Elizabethan woman who was not blessed by nature with the admired requirements set out with energy to make good by artifice. She painted her face, changed her hair-colour, plucked and darkened her eyebrows, dropped belladonna into her eyes with a feather, reddened her lips and sometimes pencilled blue veins on her partially revealed bosom.

John Donne, influential poet and clergyman, was not shocked; but most of the clergy took the line that it was wicked to attempt to improve upon the face bestowed by the Lord. Thomas Tuke asked in a treatise against face-painting: 'Will these painted women on Judgement Day be able to look up to God with a face he does not own?' But there were warnings, too, on scientific grounds: it is in fact surprising that more women did not die of lead-poisoning, caused especially by ceruse which was white lead mixed with vinegar.

A hand looking-glass was an essential for the vain by the end of the seventeenth century and long mirrors were now seen in all parts of a house. Snuff boxes often contained a small mirror on the inside of the lid.

But even the most careful woman lost her looks early in those days. Indeed, according to John Evelyn, French women were 'extremely decayed' by the age of twenty because of their 'drinking water, ill-diet and other accident'. English women aged more slowly. If past their prime at twenty, they did not actually decay until four and twenty. Scent, then as now, was bait for a man and by the beginning of the eighteenth century perfumes could be bought ready-prepared in shops.

Skin troubles of the face belonged more to women than men, and women's vanity in this respect has an alarming history from the sixteenth to the end of the eighteenth century. The Countess of Coventry and Kitty Fisher, a model for Sir Joshua Reynolds, are among several women said to have died young from the abuse of cosmetics. But what, in the words of Elizabeth Burton, was a girl to do? If she stopped painting, other women at once made disobliging remarks. Men were more restrained with cosmetics and no male deaths from their use have been recorded.

From at least 1740 onwards the dependence of the vain woman on artifice was considerable. Mrs Delaney in *The Letters* described Lady Baltimore at a royal birthday party as 'a frightful owl, her locks strutted out and most furiously greased, or rather gummed and powdered'. Cosmeticians and coiffeurs were reaching the height of their fortunes when in 1770 the following bill was tabled for the consideration of Parliament:

that all women of whatever rank, profession or degree, whether virgins, maids or widows, that shall from and after such act, impose upon, seduce and betray into matrimony, any of his Majesty's subjects by the scents, paints, cosmetic washes; artificial teeth, false hair, Spanish wool, a form of rouge pad, iron stays, hoops, high-heeled shoes and bolstered hips, shall incur the penalty of the law now in force against witchcraft and like misdemeanours, and that the marriage upon conviction shall be null and void.

But cosmetics remained a source of enjoyment and a swing-back to puritan ideals took a long time to come. Fashionable treatment of the female (and male) face was nevertheless often ridiculed, as in this article from *The Ladies' Magazine*, 1773: 'They have been told a thousand times that white hair robs their face of its expression and that rouge makes the bloom and freshness of the complexion disappear . . . They illuminate themselves after the manner of the ancient Bacchanalians and render their eyes more piercing. This custom which was in use among the most savage nations transforms the prettiest face into a painted pagoda.'[3]

An appearance as artificial as that which prevailed at this time was a matter of concern to the painters of portraits. Gainsborough recorded what he saw tolerably faithfully, but was criticized more than once for exaggerating; in 1772 it was for 'too glowing colours', and he was asked to 'borrow a little of the modest colouring of Sir Joshua Reynolds'.

The distinction of having one's portrait painted was especially valued among the courtesans, and three such ladies, painted by Gainsborough, appeared in the Royal Academy Exhibition of 1778. The *Morning Chronicle* reported that the ladies were 'very fit subjects for Mr Gainsborough's pencil, since he is rather apt to put that sort of complexion upon the countenance of his female portraits which is laughingly described, in the *School for Scandal,* as "coming in the morning and going away at night."' The approved colour scheme for the face was now a vivid red mouth and cheeks almost amounting to purple on powder-white; the hair heavily powdered. Towards the end of the eighteenth century the testimony of Reynolds is noticeably more kindly than that of Gainsborough.

At last, in the 1780s, the practice which even girls of fourteen had followed, of treating the female face with a foundation of white lead, became less common. Cheeks were safely dusted with talc and only lightly rouged, perhaps with a red leather imported from Brazil, and the colour of the lips was increased with carmine or with lipsticks made from ground and coloured plaster of Paris. Eyebrows were trimmed and blackened with lead combs or concealed behind artificialities made of mouse skin.

As for men, they continued to use cosmetics on occasion. George IV, a victim of inherited overweight and floridness, so much admired a pale skin that he used leeches in an effort to achieve a fashionable pallor. But his stoutness and habits betrayed him.

A perfectly harmless custom of sticking patches on the face to hide blemishes had begun early in the seventeenth century and continued long into the eighteenth. The patches were at first simple dots of black taffeta, but they took on new shapes and became crescent moons and stars of red silk, velvet or paper; they were generally thought practical and were, up to a certain number, ornamental.

Dyeing one's hair black to set off a rose-and-lily complexion – however obtained – was usual to judge by the number of recipes for doing so. The *Ladies' Guide* for 1700 had said that black hair could be achieved with 'gum-dye boiled with sage, myrtle, bay and beet leaves plus walnut peelings'.

Women for centuries made the pupils of their eyes appear large with belladonna – the juices of deadly nightshade. They carried with them tiny hand-mirrors and toilet sets which included an ornamental tooth-pick. They also carried scent bottles. Washing any-thing was difficult and sanitation crude, and every-thing possible was perfumed: bodies, shoes, leather screens, books and gloves. Water was by no means on tap and on Queen Victoria's accession in 1837 there

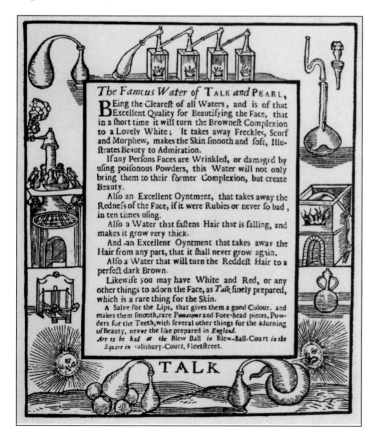

The specious advertisement of an early eighteenth-century beauty-specialist

was no bathroom in Buckingham Palace, though the Queen had a portable tub in her bedroom. George IV's marble bath at Brighton, which she inherited, was sawn up to make mantelpieces for the palace.

By the middle of the nineteenth century, the wearing of lip colouring was unusual, although rouged cheeks were often seen in good circles, as were shadowed eyes and polished finger-nails. In the 1870s social rules were growing stricter and any kind of painted face was rare except on the stage. Sarah Bernhardt went about powdered and with black lines round her eyes, but actresses were allowed a licence not extended to ladies. If a lady wanted to use cosmetics she had to do so with such discretion that the effect seemed only the slightest improvement on nature. The rich and daring secretly visited such establishments as Madame Rachel's in New Bond Street where 'Chinese Leaves for the Cheek and Lips' were offered at a high price.[4]

For a particular course of baths at Madame Rachel's the price was 100 to 1,000 guineas. In her publicity material Madame Rachel remarked: 'How frequently we find that a slight blemish on the face, otherwise divinely beautiful, has occasioned a sad and solitary life of celibacy – unloved, unblessed and ultimately unwept and unremembered.' But potential clients were assured that her expertise as a beautician would make them immune from such an end. Madame Rachel's salon, opened in 1863, was shut down within fifteen years when she received a sentence of five years' penal servitude for blackmailing a client.

William Cobbett, seemingly addressing people too poor to buy scent, spoke up in 1829 for cleanliness, which he called 'a capital ingredient; for there never yet was, and there never will be, love of any long duration, sincere and ardent love, in any man towards a filthy mate'.[5]

The second decade of the twentieth century, which saw the widespread emancipation of women, saw also a great increase in the use of cosmetics, especially sticks of rouge paste – lipsticks – and varnish for reddening the finger nails and toe nails. The increase has continued ever since and much has been learned about effective application; men often have little idea of what happens.

In a television programme of 1991 there was an explanation of why the beauty industry makes millions of pounds: it convinces the average woman that she must constantly seek personal perfection and perpetual youth. Make-up is an important status symbol, apparently, and it is not unusual for a girl or a woman to spend £500 a year on cosmetics and what is called

Making powder compacts in a French cosmetics factory. Powders are the easiest cosmetics to manufacture, the ingredients being simply dry-mixed and sifted – talc, kaolin, various oxides and chalk. To produce make-up in solid form for powder compacts, the mixture is stirred with hot water and the resultant paste is compressed and dried

'skin care'. However, the woman who is moved to slap on the make-up with a trowel is said to be making a mistake.

The buoyant state of the cosmetics industry is also indebted to the inclination of men to use more cosmetics, especially scent. The author Paul Johnson addressed this topic in a *Spectator* article of September 1991. 'Hair gel, mousse, moisturiser, hand and cold cream, even scent – often borrowed from their wives – are being furtively but daily applied to male skins . . . Like most trends it started in America.'

Television, he said, had played a big part in a change that follows 150 years of male restraint. Politicians and other celebrities discovered how make-up could improve their appearance and were 'tempted to use it off the box'. Meanwhile for the ordinary person with facial blemishes there are little sticks, like Rimmel's, recently selling at the rate of three thousand a day.

6

Teeth Like the Keyboard of a Spinet

Vanity inspired the first false teeth, those of the rich Greeks and Phoenicians, for example. They used gold wire for tying artificial teeth made of bone to adjacent natural teeth. But the Etruscans excelled at all mechanical skill with dental appliances and tomb finds show that serviceable partial dentures of bridge-work type were being worn as early as 700 BC. Gold retaining bands were kept well away from the gum line to prevent irritation, the artificial teeth resting not on the gums but on flanking teeth. Vincento Guerini, dental historian, has written that the Etruscans wore their false teeth with pride. 'Since the gold bands of which they were constructed covered a considerable part of the crowns they certainly could not have had the pretension of escaping notice . . . the wearing of false teeth was not a thing to be ashamed of; indeed it constituted a refinement only accessible to persons of means.'[1]

Above, Etruscan bridgework. Below, Phoenician false teeth wired to natural teeth

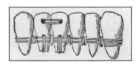

Martial, the first-century Roman writer, refers to wooden teeth: 'Maxima has three, all boxwood and as black as pitch.' Roman work at an end, the art of making false teeth barely advanced in 1600 years and nor did the art of dealing with decay. It is recorded of Queen Elizabeth that 'when she cometh in public she putteth many fine cloths into her mouth to bear out her cheeks'. Similar lip padding was used 200 years later by George Washington when hopelessly trying to look his best for a portrait now widely known from its use on stamps and coins.

At the sixteenth-century French court, restorative dentistry could be sophisticated. Henri III, once a suitor of Elizabeth, had several front teeth made of bone. He was unusually vain, colouring his face and eyes and even his ears and wearing a wig because of a disastrous attempt to dye his hair. Arthur Lufkin in his *History of Dentistry* quotes a traveller watching the morning ritual of fitting Henri's teeth: 'I saw a servant kneel before the king, take hold of his beard and pull down the lower jaw; then, opening a little bottle, he took out some small things of bone and attached them with fine wire to the adjoining teeth on either side.'

The first English book solely on dentistry, *The Operator for the Teeth*, 1685, by Charles Allen, is only slightly encouraging. 'When our decayed teeth are so far gone that whatever we do proves fruitless . . . we are not yet to despair and esteem ourselves toothless for the rest of our life: the natural want may be supplied artificially.' Allen deplored the new procedure of transplanting, pushing into the sockets of bad teeth sound teeth from another's head. At the same time he thought it might be profitable to transplant the teeth of sheep and dogs into the human jaw. From the vagueness of Allen's instructions it may be supposed that neither he nor anyone else ever carried this out.

The seventeenth-century poet Robert Herrick made false teeth seem a ridiculous vanity,[2] but by the end of the century London's 'Operators for the Teeth' were realizing that there were rich rewards to be had from supplying the vain. An advertisement in *The Ladies' Diary* of 1711 proclaims 'Artificial teeth set on so well as to eat with them, and not to be distinguished from natural, not to be taken out at night, as is by some falsely suggested, but may be worn for years together.'[3]

But the typical rows of teeth procurable rarely corrected a facial disfigurement, sometimes making it worse by enforcing an unnatural position of the lower jaw. A portrait painter working on the poet William Wordsworth thought dentures were causing distortion to the poet's face and asked him to take them out. The poorness of fit tolerated is indicated by the existence of practitioners supplying false teeth by post in exchange for a home-made wax impression.

Where expense was no object teeth made of silver, mother of pearl or enamelled copper could be requested for attaching to an ivory base. The Duchess of Portland, in a letter of 1735, describes the foppish Lord Hervey, hitherto toothless, appearing one day with 'the finest set of Egyptian pebble teeth that ever you saw'.[4] John, Lord Hervey, vice-chancellor to Queen Caroline, was at this time thirty-nine. His teeth are believed to have been agate and made in Italy.

As late as 1846 a dentist wrote that false teeth were only for the vain. 'They are too insecure in the mouth to admit of any attempt at complete mastication of food.' The vain wearers had long persevered and their dentists had been the recipients of jocular verses. William Green, dentist to George III, is celebrated in this sarcastic couplet by Charles Churchill:

Teeth white as ever teeth were seen,
Delivered from the hand of Green.

Lines to the American dentist, James Gardette, about the sweet sounds he made possible 'through Ivory's double rows', are transparently ironical.

George Washington's dental arrangements, never secure, gave him an arrestingly hollow sound. On the other side of the Atlantic, in a political attack on Lord Palmerston in the House of Commons, Disraeli was bold enough to remark that his false teeth would 'fall out of his mouth if he did not hesitate and halt so much in his speech'.

George Washington as a vain young man, without dentures, who was an inspiration to his forces. Portrait by John Trumball

Although concealment of even a good teeth-maker's work was impossible, it remained a pathetic preoccupation. Wearers and beholders observe, said a dentist, 'the most profound mystery'.[5] Queen Victoria's dentist wrote of fitting a woman with a partial row of human teeth mounted on ivory and of her return four years later with a sore mouth and the new teeth cemented to the natural ones with tartar. In her anxiety to keep her secret from every member of the family, the lady had never removed them.

With uncertain adaptation to the jaws, eighteenth-century false teeth, useless for eating, were stylized teeth comparable with stylized male wigs, and they long remained a comment-causing luxury that was best left alone. The dentist Thomas Berdmore tried hard in the late eighteenth century to make them more popular. 'Remember,' he wrote, 'that no one can excel in the art of pleasant conversation whose loss of teeth or rotten livid stumps and fallen lips destroy . . . the happy expression of the countenance.'

The first effective method of attaching an upper set to a toothless mouth, by springs fixed to the lower set, was worked out by Pierre Fauchard, a Parisian surgeon. His springs exerted a constant pressure in the mouth forcing the artificial teeth into contact with the gums. Naturally some muscular effort was needed to shut the mouth – which partially opened in repose – but at least top sets with these powerful stabilizers never fell.[6]

The great poet William Wordsworth aged forty-eight, depicted by his friend Haydon in 1818

There was no prejudice against false teeth in smarter Paris. 'Without them,' said a dentist there, 'some people cannot make any distinct and perfectly articulate sound.' Although, in the words of a contemporary observer, the replacements looked like the keyboard of a spinet, they were preferable in salon circles to bare gums.

Late eighteenth-century sets may have given confidence in talk and smiling but control by the cheeks was still needed for chewing, as there was little to stop the teeth slipping sideways. Removal on coming to the table remained usual, though men put their teeth back to improve their enunciation over the port. Port had a rapidly darkening effect on ivory and indeed the vanity of wearing ivory teeth turned into something unpleasant after about a year, so blackened and spoiled did they become.

In the 1790s there came news of false teeth with base and teeth made in one solid piece of shiny, rot-proof porcelain. These were the celebrated mineral paste dentures for which Nicholas Dubois de Chemant of Paris had no difficulty in getting testimonials. Edward Jenner, discoverer of vaccination, wrote one; so did the president of the Royal Society of Medicine in Paris. De Chemant prospered. The Paris Faculty of Medicine pronounced that his dentures 'united the qualities of beauty, solidity and comfort to the exigencies of hygiene'; King Louis XVI granted him an inventor's patent and General Comte de Martagne, aged eighty-two, wrote a verse:

> When time has stripped our armoury bare
> Dubois steps in with subtle heed;
> New grinders and new cutters gives;
> With his we laugh, with his we feed.
> Long live Chemant, friend in need.

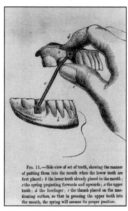

Instructions for inserting false teeth on springs, 1851. An error could render the springs ineffective and prevent the false teeth from staying even roughly in place

George Washington aged sixty-four as painted by Gilbert Stuart in 1796, when his looks had been damaged by crude false teeth. Washington wore cotton rolls in his mouth for the portrait in an attempt to soften the protrusion of the lower set

De Chemant in fact proceeded to live long in London and not Paris because of the nuisance of the French Revolution. For extra strength his teeth were not separated along their length, merely shaded. Although immediately striking the eye as art work, they and their pink porcelain gums at least looked shiny and fresh. Naturally grinding surfaces lost their glaze, as other dentists sternly pointed out, and there were unfortunate cases of dentures cracking in half, sometimes in the mouth. But what really brought the craze to an end was the inability of de Chemant's imitators to make them fit properly so that patients had a slightly grotesque appearance.

Although de Chemant's full sets of mineral paste could not after all fulfil a dream, the freedom from decay did stimulate work on individual porcelain teeth for attaching to bases of ivory or metal. But these looked most artificial and a London firm was still supplying ivory blocks for false teeth as recently as 1875. The demand continued, too, for human teeth plundered from the corpses of vault and battlefield.

Provided they were steady, human teeth deceived. But in *King Solomon's Mines* (Rider Haggard, 1885) Captain Good's vanity concerning his mouth did not check a habit of playing with his teeth in a way which clearly showed they were not his own. A nervous trick of plucking at the top set which was supported by springs electrified a savage tribe encountered in Africa.

Accidental malfunction of springs could be worse than inconvenient, since without them few sets would hold up even in conversation. The Victorian lady hated to be caught without a second pair, and booklets of the time gave instructions on how to avoid a mishap.

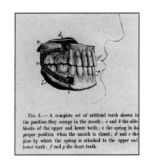

Fig. 5. — A complete set of artificial teeth shown in the position they occupy in the mouth; *a* and *b* the side-blocks of the upper and lower teeth; *c* the spring in its proper position when the mouth is closed; *d* and *e* the pins by which the spring is attached to the upper and lower teeth; *f* and *g* the front teeth.

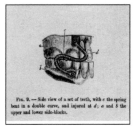

Fig. 9. — Side view of a set of teeth, with *c* the spring bent in a double curve, and injured at *d*; *a* and *b* the upper and lower side-blocks.

Correct and incorrect positioning for retaining springs, according to a handbook of 1851. "If a spring should get in the position shown on the right, (below) it will be so damaged, if not absolutely broken, that its action will ever after be imperfect"

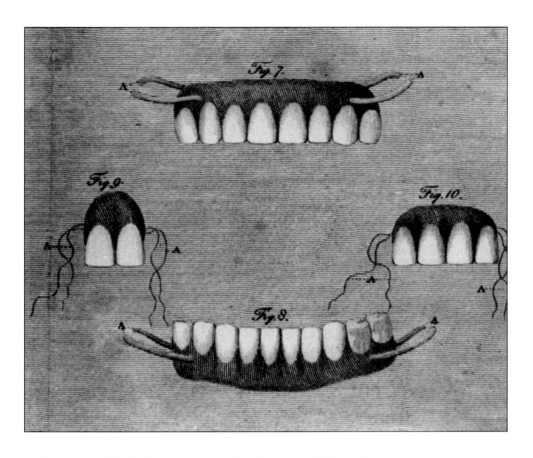

However ill-fitting a person's plate might be, at least with springs he was safe while talking. Springs were economical, too; there was no need to have a new set made because of gum shrinkage and people took pride in managing dentures that were forty years old. As recently as the 1970s there were a few elderly people with teeth retained by coil springs of stainless steel, help being often needed for the morning adjustment.

Pierre Fauchard fitted springs, knowing nothing of atmospheric pressure as a means of retention. And since his upper sets were formed in a brief horseshoe shape just like lower sets, there was little opportunity for it to assert itself (plates covering the whole roof of the mouth, as today, were barely even thought of until

Partial sets of porcelain teeth for hooking or tying into position, dating from the late eighteenth century. Those tied were useful only as decoration

the 1830s). But Fauchard took infinite care with the fit of his carved ivory bases, and was able to report having three times in his career made upper sets that would stay in place without springs.

An insecure plateless upper set of the early nineteenth century, the whole carved from a single block of ivory

In writing of them he admits the need of support from the cheeks and the lower teeth to bring them back into place. His advice to other dentists was to make such sets very light and not to expect them to do much more than improve the appearance and pronunciation. Only a very few people, he said, were able to wear them. Most likely, a few had learned the trick of balancing their false teeth with their tongues.

Forty years after Fauchard's death, a satisfactory springless top set made by James Gardette of Philadelphia was hailed as a dental triumph; he realized why it worked (because of its plate) and became established as the discoverer of the use of atmospheric pressure in dentistry.

In England it was not until around 1835 that the notion of suction plates began to be talked about. When occasionally asked for them, dentists did their best to oblige, but often without having much faith in them, or even an understanding of the principle. W.H. Mortimer in his *Essay on Artificial Teeth* (1845) offered his considered opinion on teeth 'kept in by suction . . . without any fastening whatever . . . I cannot, I confess, understand how they answer. One thing I have invariably observed . . . is that the gums are in a constant state of irritation and inflammation.'

In the 1860s and 1870s false-teeth advertisements in the newspapers still proclaimed atmospheric pressure as a marvellous new dental invention: 'No springs,' they announced, 'or any other fastening required.' Fastidious patients often found it an embarrassing invention that worked only sometimes, and failed completely at meals. The actual teeth tended to be so ill-arranged that even a close-fitting denture was easily dislodged.

Springs rarely caused injury, but by the end of the century they came to be supplied with reluctance; dentists saw them as a reflection on their ability to do close-fitting work. Often their plates were failures and patients neglected, or could not afford, to go back for adjustments following the normal shrinking of the mouth tissues. Thus began, around 1890, the long era of the dancing top set.

Crowns today transform the mouths of the vain and the sensible who have not suffered full loss of teeth. More or less efficient crowns date only from the beginning of the twentieth century. The satisfaction to be derived from their ability to improve one's smile comes out in these letters to his parents from President Roosevelt in youth, a man whose proper sense of vanity lasted throughout life.

May 19, 1902

After lunch I went to the dentist, and am now minus my front tooth. He cut it off very neatly and painlessly, took impressions of the root and space, and is having the porcelain tip baked. I hope to have it put in next Friday, and in the meantime I shall avoid all society.

May 28, 1902

My tooth is no longer a dream, it is an accomplished fact. It was put in on Friday and is in perfect form, color, lustre, texture etc. I feel like a new person and have already been proposed to by three girls.

Progress in the making of crowns and bridges was retarded for lack of a grinding machine and of a cement that would stay hard in the mouth. Thus, although by the 1880s almost everyone could obtain almost passable full dental plates, even the rich would be fitted with crowns as crude and impermanent as those made in the days of Fauchard. The proper preparation of roots was barely possible with hand instruments.

Some dentists were still fixing their crowns with pegs of hickory wood; these were pushed into the root canals and held there until moisture caused them to swell and become tight. Sometimes roots split. According to a textbook 'A pivot of the toughest wood is inserted, so prepared to enter each cavity without much force, where it will soon swell and make the tooth very permanent and durable . . . The pivot may be renewed by the patient when necessary.'[7]

Most people with partial loss preferred fixed replacements because, unlike dentures, which usually slipped, they did not carry the full stigma of false teeth. Dentists liked them too: they were more profitable and, thanks to a new cement, they could be made to stay in place even when poorly made. Consequently all roots were saved to hold a tooth or bridge. What rarely took place, even in the early twentieth century, was any aseptic filling of these roots.

Trouble followed, especially in America where the chief mechanical improvements originated. Dr Bremmer writes in his *Story of Dentistry* 'Frequently the teeth under the well-constructed bridges would abscess and develop pus-discharging fistulae, but few dentists were disturbed by these manifestations . . .

The fact that teeth were intimately connected with the blood stream seems to have escaped the attention not only of the dentist but of the physician as well.'

The showdown came in 1911 and Dr Bremmer described it. The situation was such that the English physician William Hunter publicly accused American dentistry of contributing to the ill health of the people. Dr Hunter, practising among the rich of London, had several patients in bed with ailments he was at a loss to diagnose. Some of them had in their mouths extensive restoration work which was dirty and built on unhealthy looking roots.

To give anything a try, he ordered the removal of all bridges and of the roots holding them. Most patients objected. The work had been expensive and removing it meant disfigurement and more difficult chewing. But of the few who obeyed, a significant number began to get rapidly better. In his printed observations Dr Hunter described the cleverly-made bridges as 'mausoleums of gold over a mass of sepsis', a phrase given publicity by the Press.

Dentists were indignant, but the medical profession became seriously interested: here was a fresh thought about the association existing between the teeth, the gums and the bloodstream, and almost overnight doctors started to blame the teeth for any illness they could not readily diagnose. Out the teeth must come.

Bewilderment set in when it was found that wholesale extractions did not always bring recovery. Young people as well as old were having their teeth pulled out, regardless of their illness, and not enjoying a return to health. Their mouths were wrecked, vanity became difficult. The widespread use of X-ray equipment at last brought sanity: films showed whether a dead tooth with a filled root was healthy or diseased.

Dentists learned that only certain dead teeth can be safely used for restoration purposes, their pulp not having lost contact with the blood circulation.

But a great need for false teeth continued through the thirties and beyond, and those with money could wear teeth which looked almost natural (those without money, or vanity, wore embarrassingly wobbly teeth). Dentists had become more canny and recorded the exact positions of the natural teeth before extraction; they also built up their plates to restore spoiled contours of the mouth.

Often the whole face could be improved by dental attention. A person's chin gets nearer the nose with age, but much can be done by adding bulk to sets of artificial teeth; a sad expression can be changed into a serene expression.

A few decades ago it was usual to let a toothless patient wait months while the gums healed, but apart

Advertisement for false teeth, 1857. Even the worst false teeth would push out a person's lips

This Plate represents the Face of a Lady deprived of her Teeth, their loss occasioning that close approximation of the nose & chin so Characteristic of Old Age

This Plate represents the same Face restored to its original & Youthful appearance, by the aid of Artificial Teeth as supplied by

M.r Thomas Howard

from the embarrassment of being toothless there was the drawback of certain things happening to the mouth during the waiting period which made it difficult eventually to fit new teeth. Too often gums had become flattened, and facial lines had appeared which no dentist could iron out.

There need be no interval today between having teeth out and new ones in. The dentist can make models of the gums with the natural teeth still in place and prepare new teeth in advance of extraction. He puts them in within minutes of the removal of the old ones. It has been known for a person to make the exchange without his own family suspecting it; he explains refusal to eat grilled steak by remarking that he has just had a tooth out.

It sounds painful to wear a hard set of false teeth on top of sore gums, but in practice the plate shields these from the irritation of tongue movements and food, reduces the inevitable slight bleeding and allows soothing lotions to stay where they are needed instead of being washed away. Healing is quicker, too, and the bone ridge better formed. Patients find that instead of it seeming to be suspended, the lower jaw has a comfortable resting place; and vanity is possible.

Current methods of making false teeth have become standard. The dentist takes impressions of the upper and lower jaws and makes casts of them by pouring plaster of Paris into the impressions; sets of teeth on plates could be built on these reproductions, but instead they are used for making facsimiles in artificial stone. The resultant plates fit perfectly, but the teeth of the two sets must be adjusted so that they can grind correctly. Although teeth of porcelain can look marvellously life-like, most people prefer teeth of the softer acrylic resin because they make no noise on being brought together and thus placate vanity.

7

Transplanting Teeth and Other Tricks

Vanity asserts itself when a single front tooth is lost. The effect can be as upsetting as when a whole row disappears. The barbarous operation of transplanting formerly offered a way of replacing front teeth. The decayed tooth was drawn and immediately a sound tooth from another mouth was pushed into the socket.

The transplanting of human teeth was referred to by Paré in 1564 and by Charles Allen, with distaste, in 1685. In the late eighteenth century, publicity turned transplanting into almost a craze. Some dentists did as many as six transplants in a week, although with varying success. The better ones – since disease was occasionally transferred – made some attempt to check that those who offered their teeth were free from infection; and it was thought wise to rinse the newly extracted good tooth in warm water. Under the best circumstances, a transplant would settle down in a month or two and remain firm for three, even five years.

Although a few voices were raised at the cruelty of depriving the poor of useful teeth, no one was surprised that poverty should impel them to earn a little money in this way. There seems never to have been a serious lack of volunteers. Laetitia-Matilda Hawkins writes in her *Memoirs* (1824), that the celebrated Lady

Hamilton once resolved to sell some of her front teeth: she was then young Emma Hart, out of a situation and destitute. On her way to the dentist, however, she met an old fellow servant who persuaded her to resort to a less creditable method of making money.

The writings of John Hunter in the eighteenth century were largely responsible for the limited popularity of transplanting. His stature as a general surgeon was such that people paid attention to what he said about dentistry. Hunter experimentally undertook numerous transplantings, a task which he considered, unlike supervision of false-teeth making, within the province of a surgeon.[1]

He advised operators to have several people in attendance. If the first person's tooth did not suit, the corresponding one from the next should be instantly pulled and tried in. Once a reasonable fit had been achieved, the transplanted tooth had to be immobilized by tying it to the adjacent tooth.

An etching by Thomas Rowlandson (1787) gives an idea of the preposterous procedure. The dentist is shown extracting a tooth from a young chimney sweep sitting beside a vain and fashionably dressed lady whose jaw is about to receive it. She waits with smelling salts held to her nose. On her right the next offerer, a girl, sits with clenched hands while an assistant examines her mouth. Behind her, a patient who has been treated regards the result without enthusiasm in a glass. At the far left, two raggedly dressed young people, holding their aching jaws, are leaving the room. The little girl looks down at the coins taken in payment for her teeth.

There is something especially pathetic in the way the very young were exploited. But Hunter strongly recommended the teeth of young healthy subjects as those most likely to transplant well. He admitted that by no means every case succeeded. What he meant by success is probably exemplified by the following case history of an American patient of his which has been written up by Dr Menzies Campbell in *The Dental Practitioner.*

Three lower front teeth were skilfully transplanted and in a short time became quite firm. Five years later they had worked loose. The patient consulted the Philadelphia dentist James Gardette, who found that the upper teeth were biting on them too heavily and causing inflammation. He filed down the transplanted teeth and prescribed an astringent mouthwash. Within two months they were tight again, remaining so for a further five years, and subsequently staying in place for several years in a loose condition.

Transplanting spread from Europe to America in

The vanity of transplanting teeth commonly involved exploitation of the young and poor. The dentist is Bartholomew Ruspini, surgeon dentist to the Prince of Wales who also serves, according to a notice on his wall, the Empress of Russia. Etching by Thomas Rowlandson, *Transplanting of Teeth*, 1787

TRANSPLANTING OF TEETH

the latter years of the eighteenth century, a French surgeon called Pierre Le Mayeur having a lot to do with this by electing to specialize in the operation. He arrived in America in 1781 and within five years was prosperous enough to establish a stable of horses. Le Mayeur treated George Washington several times, staying overnight at Mount Vernon for the purpose. There is no record of his having transplanted teeth for Washington, but it is known that he transplanted four front teeth and one eye tooth for his aide, Colonel Varick. Washington remarked in a letter to Varick: 'I have been staggered in my belief in the efficacy of transplantation of living teeth.'

For several years from 1782 Le Mayeur regularly advertised in the papers:

Doctor LE MAYEUR. FRONT TEETH. Any person disposed to part with their FRONT TEETH may receive Two guineas for each Tooth, on applying to No. 28, Maiden Lane (New York).

But Le Mayeur did not always take advantage of offers. There is the following anecdote in the *Daily Advertiser* for 28 January 1789 in which he is the dentist referred to:

In the severe winter of 1783, which was a time of general distress in New York, an aged couple found themselves reduced to their last stick of wood. They were supported by a daughter, who found herself unable to secure wood, fuel or provision. She accidentally heard of a dentist who advertised that he would give 3 guineas for every sound tooth . . . He, affected by her tears, refused to proceed and presented her with 10 guineas instead.

In the *New York Independent Journal* of 18 December 1784 he announced: 'Dr Le Mayeur has transplanted one hundred and twenty three teeth since last June, and assures the public that not one of his operations has failed of the wished-for success.'

The latter assertion need not be the blatant lie it appears at first sight. As Le Mayeur was writing within a few months of the operations, it is quite possible that in the interval none of the transplanted teeth had gone wrong to the point of having to come out – or if some had, that he had not yet heard about it. And the phrase 'wished-for success' is ingenious: Le Mayeur would have been aware that with certain transplantings a brief life was all the success he personally could wish for.

Viewed in this way, Le Mayeur's claim can even be reconciled with a report of 1824, some twenty years after his death, written by his colleague Gardette:

> In the course of my practice I had occasion to extract at least fifty of these transplanted teeth – most of them without an instrument, with my fingers only – and to replace them by artificial teeth. Many accidents occur to the transplanted teeth, while they are growing firm, and some never get firmly fixed in the sockets at all.

However, Gardette was writing for a thesis: he called his paper 'Observations on the Transplantation of Teeth, which tend to show the impossibility of the Success of that Operation'. His argument is that transplanting could only work, as replacing a tooth in its own socket worked (replantation), if the root of the transplant was exactly the length, size and shape of the defective one; and as this was a matter the dentist had to decide without seeing either, it was impossible.

In England, Berdmore, dentist to George III, considered that several successful transplantings were really replantings: the operator had quickly filled and repaired an extracted bad tooth and then put it back, charging the fee for a transplanted tooth. He said he had seen the evidence of this deception in the mouths of his patients.[2]

It would be seemly to report that transplanting quickly died out as the nineteenth century wore on and as false teeth improved. But although the mini-craze was over, some rich people, especially women, continued to insist on the operation. As late as 1919 in *Dental Surgery and Pathology* J.F. Colyer sets out the method of performing it. The patient to receive the transplanted tooth:

> is first operated upon, as little injury as possible being inflicted, and the bleeding from the socket arrested as far as possible. The tooth to be transplanted is next removed from the other patient and immediately transferred to the vacant socket and forced well into place.

However, Colyer, who was examiner in dentistry to the Royal College of Surgeons, does put forward the moral objection that 'the teeth to be transplanted are usually obtained from the poorer classes, [very often a person's housemaid] and opines that, considering everything, the practice is to be condemned'. Since Colyer's day the only sort of transplanting that has been publicly discussed is the more respectable procedure of shifting teeth about within the same mouth. Replanting teeth dislodged by accident remains accepted practice; it almost always succeeds if resorted to without delay.

Transplanting teeth was just one of many bad kinds of treatment given to people *in extremis*. The upsetting effect of tooth-loss or of gross decay made it easy in Victorian times – and later times – for the least trained person to attract patients by putting an enormous sign above his door; tyros and imposters advertised alongside the roughly reputable, using the same words. But training was hard to get, no dental school existing in England until 1858. Apprenticeship was the only procedure.

Honest dentists campaigned endlessly against the charlatans ensnaring the vain and people who were

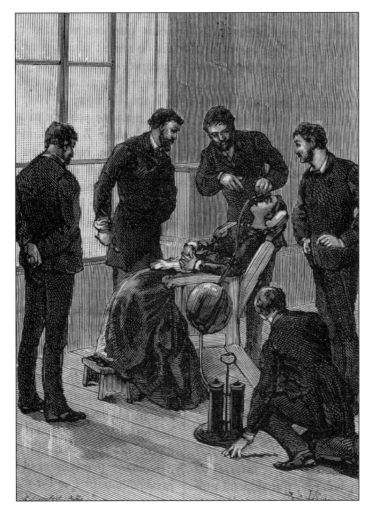

Late nineteenth-century dental treatment, using anaesthetics

suffering. John Gray of the Royal College of Surgeons wrote in 1838: 'The greatest mischief inflicted by quacks is the odium and distrust their malpractices bring upon the profession they invade. Scarcely a week passes in which I am not consulted by some person who has been entrapped.'[3]

Nineteenth-century stories abound. There was the gentleman of Colchester, needing two fillings and one extraction, who was beguiled to visit a travelling 'dental expert' whose proper occupation was baking. The dental expert observed that it was fortunate his patient had not delayed because in another week filling his teeth would have become impossible. While mixing silver filings and mercury he spoke of a clientele which seemed to include most of the nobility. The filling poured in, he seated his patient on the floor and gripped his head between the knees. The bad tooth came out after a prolonged struggle and was accompanied by the tooth next to it. The dental expert said this was good as both teeth were ossified: he hoped the operation had not hurt too much.[4]

The Dentists' Act of 1878 established a register of dentists but failed to make it unlawful for people without qualifications to practise. So long as the unregistered did not call themselves dentists they could be 'dental experts' and put up signs reading Dental Parlour or Dental Surgery. Some of these augmented newspaper advertisements with posters at railway stations; some pushed handbills into the windows of carriages and into the letter boxes of big houses.

Although taking trouble to decorate their windows with specimen sets of false teeth, most operators, qualified and unqualified, worked in humble alleys. This may have been partly to spare the blushes of vain patients anxious not to be observed making their visits, but it did nothing to enhance the status of dentistry.

Some of the more ambitious London dentists on the other hand (again, 'dental experts' as well as registered practitioners), paid handsomely to rent rooms at addresses smart enough for anyone to enter with dignity. Such rooms were attended by footmen in livery and were furnished with Turkish carpets, rosewood furniture, magnificent candelabra and expensive paintings and books.

In these surroundings the rich and the vain were prepared to pay the frock-coated dentist enormous sums for his false teeth. Dr Menzies Campbell, whose collection of old dental anecdotes is unrivalled, describes in *Dentistry Then and Now* how a smart mid-nineteenth-century dentist handled the sale of a full set fitted with human front teeth. It had taken his assistant, Charles, between two and three weeks to carve and was for a smartly dressed elderly duchess:

> The dentist received her graciously. When she was seated in the dental chair, he had the audacity to emphasize, in Charles's presence, that both of them had worked assiduously for two months on her very difficult dentures. After viewing the restorations from various angles, he expressed the firm belief that they were 'the cream of perfection'. He next handed her ladyship a mirror to enable her to confirm this. The verdict was 'Well, Mr X, you have renewed my youth: they are just lovely'. . . . Mr X informed her that his fee was £1,000 which she joyfully paid. Later he proceeded downstairs to tell Charles what he had charged and to give him £10.[5]

Overcharging, which provided some dentists with a reputed £20,000 a year, was of course encouraged by patients' money-snobbishness, taking the best to be the most expensive.

Dr Menzies Campbell writes thus of the typical early twentieth-century quack dentist with a huge brass plate beside his door:

> An untrained woman in a nurse's uniform received callers and assured them of highly skilled attention. When a person requiring dentures had been escorted into the consulting-room, he was asked what price he was prepared to pay. Should a guinea be mentioned, the quack produced a clumsy specimen with ugly dark teeth, remarking that this was the cheapest, but there were others much better. No denture was ever inserted until its entire cost had been liquidated.

In the 1920s and '30s it was apparently regular pracitce not to allow a caller to leave until some treatment had been undertaken. Extractions began with a central front tooth since the unsightly gap ensured a return visit.

8

Priests who Knocked off Wigs

The ancient Egyptians used wigs which were highly stylized and were worn on formal or festive occasions; they can rarely have been meant to hide natural defects since it was common to make the head bald artificially by shaving it.

From at least 3,000 BC, it appears from ancient paintings, both men and women of rank wore wigs with their full dress. The wigs were made of human hair, vegetable fibre or grass and consisted of neat plaits and braids. Around 1,000 BC they became large enough to give the vain wearer a top-heavy appearance.

Queen Isimkhets, *c.* 900 BC, had a vast wig. Hers was one of fifteen in the Cairo Museum analysed chemically in 1930 by Alfred Lucas. It had been described as made of hair mixed with sheep's wool. Mr Lucas found human hair only. He examined two wigs of Roman date and discovered that one was made of date-palm fibre and the other of grass. To hold the work in position all wigs had been treated with a wax identified by its melting point as beeswax.[1]

Wigs were fashionable among Roman women for everyday use according to contemporary Roman writers. They offered the vain an easy way of seeming blonde in a land of dark heads, and numerous wigs

Schist statue of Queen Khamerernebty II, and her husband, showing Old Kingdom style of dress and wig, of about 2530 BC

Lady Werel on the tomb of Ramose, Thebes, showing a New Kingdom style of wig

were made with flaxen hair collected from the conquered Germanic natives of Northern Europe. These wigs would not have looked life-like to a modern eye – but neither would natural hair, so rigid was the manner of crimping it.

In general Roman men put on wigs only to hide baldness and did not pretend to an unlikely colour like flaxen. To go by the workmanship of wigs to be seen in museums, it was possible for a man's wig to look life-like. The wigmaker did not have to simulate a parting or a hair line – both difficult – since it was customary for male hair to be combed forward like that of Julius Caesar. The work was good enough to be embarrassing if accidentally exposed. However, a few bald men were so absurd as to have black hair painted on their skulls. Martial, the first-century Roman writer, rudely said in a note to one such man: 'You have no occasion for a barber for your head; you may shave yourself better, Phoebus, with a sponge.'

Wigs had a place in the wardrobes of several Roman emperors. Caligula put one on to disguise himself while prowling at night and Caracalla, according to Herodian, ingratiated himself on visiting a Danube-side settlement by wearing not only German dress but also a blond wig trimmed in local style. Caracalla's everyday hair, as shown on his coins, was the inspiration for ladies' fashion wigs of the 1790s featuring curls that resembled sausages.

Some wigs of the great Romans would have been no more than hat-like adornments to be slipped on and off at whim. How much they were used in this way is guesswork. But it is not incredible to read in Evelyn Waugh's historical novel *Helena*, 1950, that the Emperor Constantine received his mother at the

Palatine in a small green wig. 'My dear boy, what have you got on your head?'

'Don't you like it?' he asked anxiously. 'Do you think it makes me look pale?'

The early Christian Church tried to smother the vanity of wig-wearing, especially among women. To the early fathers embellishment of the head with false hair was an affront to chastity, an enticement to illicit pleasures. Clement of Alexandria (first century) declared it was impossible for anyone in a wig to receive a priest's blessing, this being unable to pass through a stranger's hair. It appears that women were sporting their false hair in a way that was both alluring and detectable by the clergy. For centuries the Roman Church condemned the use of such hair and in 692 the Council of Constantinople actually excommunicated a number of wig-wearing Christians.

By the twelfth century women were avoiding accusations of immodesty by wearing a decorous fabric head-dress, but men continued to get into trouble over their hair. St Anselm, a twelfth-century Archbishop of Canterbury, was uncompromising about the vanity of young men with long hair and once put several aristocratic youths on penance, refusing absolution until they agreed to be close shorn.

The French kings who had traditionally enjoyed the privilege of having hair as long as they liked were now falling in with the wishes of the Church and wearing it short. It was not until the end of the sixteenth century that the Church's influence on hairstyles ceased to be effective.

In Elizabethan times great ladies found it pleasanter to keep an array of wigs than sit through the treatments needed for maintaining all the curls then fashionable. Thus began the first English vogue for the female wig of vanity. It was Queen Elizabeth I herself who started this vogue, possessing as she did, a large number of neatly curled wigs.

King Louis XIV was responsible for the final triumph of the wig for male use in France; as a young man he was happy with his own abundant hair and scorned wigs, but baldness at thirty-two made him change his mind. His wigs were voluminous, majestic and black. Only in extreme age would he permit a sprinkling of powder to suggest a becoming greyness and his barber used to boast that he would crop the heads of any number of Frenchmen to keep the king's head properly covered.

But embarrassments to do with wig-wearing continued. In 1690 Jean-Baptiste Thiers, parish priest of Champrond, published a book of 550 pages about wigs and the clergy, its purpose to expose practices he thought wicked. The book offers amusing stories of how much priests spent at the barber's; of priests wearing their best wigs in the drawing-room and inferior wigs in church; of priests turned out of their livings for wig-wearing only to be welcomed by the easy-going bishop of another diocese. There are descriptions of comical scenes in vestries with wigged priests preparing themselves for the altar and other priests trying to knock their wigs off.[2]

The Archbishop of Reims believed he had settled the dispute by decreeing that in some circumstances wigs could be worn by infirm priests, though not at the altar. One result was that a vain priest would keep his wig on until within feet of the altar and then hand it to an assistant.

Concerned as they were with a flattering frame for the face, some men merely sewed bunches of hair round the rims of their hats. But Englishmen and their

King Louis XIV in maturity. He was responsible for the final triumph of the wig for male use in France. In his heavily populated Palace of Versailles, appearances were all important

clergy were ready for the great wig-wearing fashion which came with the Restoration in 1660. The admired French wigs can be compared with floridly carved high-back chairs; like the uprights of these the long locks of hair were formed in barley sugar twists.

Although hygiene had little to do with the start of male wig-wearing vanity, it was certainly a factor in keeping it going. With uncertain soaps, hair-cleaning was difficult and the removal of lice and nits impossible. A shaved head and a few wigs meant the head need never itch for long. Nor need hairdressing take place on one's head.[3]

Samuel Pepys, a pleasantly vain person, offers in his diaries a good account of what it was like for a young man to be confronted with the fashion for full-bottom wigs. He was thirty and anxious to fit himself for mixing with the eminent. His barber, Jervas, kept on trying to persuade him to have his own luxurious hair cut off and one day invited him to try the effect of false hair. 'I did try,' Pepys writes, 'two or three borders and periwigs, meaning to wear one; and yet I have no stomach for it; but that the pains of keeping my own hair clean is so great.' He also speculates on 'the trouble that I foresee will be in wearing them'.

At length he succumbed, and towards the end of 1663 submits himself for the full hair-cutting ordeal. 'It went a little to my heart to part with it at present, but it being over and my periwig on, I paid Jervas £3 for it: and away went he with my own hair to make up another of.'

He is diffident to start with, and grateful for the admiring comments of his wife and maidservants. However, going to church in the wig for the first time 'did not prove so strange as I was afraid it would'. It is not necessary to turn many pages in his diary to find him well satisfied with his changed appearance and happily choosing a better wig box.

In April 1665 Pepys is briefly wigless again, having sent his wig to Jervas for cleaning and repairs. He writes that 'having suffered my own hair to grow long, in order to wear it, I find the convenience of periwigs is so great, that I have cut off all short again and will keep to periwigs'.

Later on he becomes rather worried about the origin of the bought hair. He records on a Sunday in September 1665: 'Up, and put on my coloured silk suit, very fine, and my new periwig, bought a good while since, but durst not wear, because the plague was in Westminster when I bought it; and it is a wonder what will be the fashion, after the plague is done, as to periwigs, for nobody will dare to buy any hair for fear of the infection, that it had been cut off the heads of people dead of the plague.'

Nevertheless the following year Pepys bought two wigs at once. They were expensive at £4 10s. the pair. He described them as 'mighty fine; indeed too fine, I thought for me'. One of them 'made a great show' in church.

Seventeenth-century household accounts reveal to what a large extent wig-vanity augmented expenditure on apparel. In 1672 the Earl of Bedford's bill from the Woburn wigmaker came to £54 10s. He had four new wigs in the year, ranging in price from £6 to £20; one at £10 was described as 'a periwig for riding'.[4]

Under James II wigs became even bigger, each requiring the growth from several heads. They had two great horns of hair rising up in front on each side of a parting and gave rise to the term 'bigwig' for a wealthy or important person.

Women, during most of the seventeenth century,

allowed their hair to look rather like the men's. Conventions about one style being feminine and another masculine barely existed. When men took to hanging side locks, so did women; and in the latter part of the century, both sexes arranged their hair, natural or false, in twin peaks on the top of the head. But a fashion peculiar to women, inspired by Italy, was to pluck a high dome-like forehead, and decorate it with thin, wispy curls. This rudimentary fringe sprang from a transverse parting: behind it the hair was strained back to form a bun.

Eighteenth-century wigs of vanity were worn with so casual a panache they could be lifted in public to

A lady's vanity wig blows off, pictured in a late eighteenth-century engraving

scratch the shaven head. They were taken off as a matter of course before fisticuffs: hence the expression 'keep your hair on'.[5]

A wig was warming for men labouring in winter weather and Pehr Kalm, a Swede visiting England in 1748 noted in *Visit to England* that wigs were worn by labourers out in the fields. It is likely that Kalm was in fact writing only of men on particular estates where the wigs for the squire and his household were so often changed that used ones were distributed among outside workers.

At night men in easy circumstances liked to wear a soft nightcap. Next morning they would go on wearing it while in a state called undress and while being attended to by a servant. The *London Connoisseur* remarked in 1754:

> The gentlemen must have their toilettes set out with washes, perfumes and cosmetics; and will spend a whole morning in scenting their linen, dressing their hair and arching their eyebrows.

A lady might buy a periwig for her little page or a man for his young son (essential for a portrait), but in general wigs were not for children. It was, however, a matter for comment if a boy of seventeen was still wearing his own hair. Men wore wigs of natural colours until about 1714 – in a variety of styles – when it became customary to bleach them or apply powder. Powdering, ideally a job for an attendant, was done with bellows or a large powder puff. A room called a wig closet might be set aside for the work. Even the humble clergyman Parson Woodforde was so vain as to powder his wig, recording in 1789: 'For a powder puff for my Wiggs pd 2s'. White was the preferred colour for powder: it eliminated at a stroke one of the signs of age and went well with any face.

Wigs of vanity were a thing of the past by about 1800, partly because of a huge tax on powder, though some whose own hair was sparse, a not unusual condition after years of wig-wearing, felt obliged to conceal the fact. In John Macdonald's *Memoirs of an Eighteenth-century Footman* there is an account of James Coutts, the banker, having tried twenty servants in one month before finding a man who could dress him to his liking. He wore what is now called a hair-piece to supplement his own hair. 'It required,' said Macdonald (who got the job), 'a person that understood the business of wig-making. When he was dressed no person could tell there was anything but his own hair . . .'[6]

The move away from wigs in the 1770s had greatly upset the great band of wigmakers; many of them, with no work to do, were going through acute hardship. In February of 1765 the wigmakers of London actually petitioned George III, drawing his attention to distress following 'the decline of the trade occasioned by the present mode of men in all stations wearing their own hair', and begging him to bring back the wig. If the wigmakers' petition had nothing to do with male wigs briefly coming back in the late 1770s, their movement in procession to St James's caused a memorable stir.

As the wigmakers marched, it was noticed, according to both Horace Walpole and Press accounts of the day, that most of them were not themselves wearing wigs; and the sight so affected sections of the watching mob that wigless barbers were seized.

By the early nineteenth century it was correct for gentlemen to wear their own hair short: a mode

Quantities of false hair were mixed with the natural to create this style of the late eighteenth century

which those who lived in great houses would not, however, permit for their footmen. For these the wig lingered on and was replaced by powdered hair which lasted, for the smartest footmen, until around 1900. In the 1880s a silk bow would be fixed at the back of the neck of the coat to represent the bow of a non-existent wig. But as late as 1886, according to an article of that year in the *Hairdressers' Weekly Journal* there were still a few coachmen and servants in livery who wore wigs.

None of the abuse to which wearers of wigs were subjected in America checked the fashion there. In the southern colonies wigs came to be worn almost as generally as in England – by blacksmiths, innkeepers and bricklayers as well as by rich Virginian planters and clergymen. To start with, wigs were ordered from London, but local barbers set about making themselves familiar with wigmaking. Such was the demand for wigs that numbers of London wigmakers emigrated with a view to practising their craft more profitably in the American colonies. Here is a typical advertisement in a New York paper of 1761:

Morrison, peruke maker from London, dresses ladies' and gentlemen's hair in the politest taste. He has a choice parcel of human, horse and goat's hair to dispose of.

'On a Saturday afternoon,' writes Leonard E. Fisher, historian of the American wigmakers, 'it was not unusual to see scores of wigmakers' apprentices dashing through the narrow streets of Boston, or any other early American city, rushing to deliver the freshly curled and powdered wigs belonging to the great and near-great men of the day.'

The era of men's wigs as part of dress came to an end in America at about the same time as in England. The wigmaking business in fact declined steadily after the War of Independence had been won in 1783. As in France, a new way of life was beginning.

It was in America that an extraordinary fashion for wigs of vanity started in 1958, inspired by a story in *Life* about the Carita sisters who were making wigs to match Givenchy dresses. Proceeds from the sale of wigs rose between 1860 and 1970 from $4 million to $500 million. When a Florida firm announced courses in selling, fitting and maintenance of wigs, two thousand people wanted to attend a single seminar.

In the spring of 1966 the London *Daily Express* had a write-up of a wig known as the 'Smoochy' which was 'designed for the not-so-pretty girl'. It was silver-grey and covered half the face, including one eye. It was so glamorous, said the *Express* reporter, that any slight plainness still showing did not matter.

In 1966 several papers carried a story about a shopkeeper, aged fifty-six, of Harlow in Essex, whose wig shrank after being tinted by a local barber at the latter's suggestion. He sued, contending that not being able to wear his wig added twenty years to his apparent age. When he placed it on his head in court, the judge agreed that it could not be worn without embarrassment and awarded him damages of £90. The barber remarked: 'It was a shocking fit in the first place and the carroty brown colour was ridiculous. I thought it looked better after my treatment.'

Vanity about his hair was the undoing of a Basingstoke burglar. He was readily traced by the police as a result of losing his partial wig in a scuffle at the scene of a burglary. He had invested in a hair

The Duke of Marlborough's coachman, still wearing a wig in about 1900

piece of such quality that the maker had stamped it with a serial number.[7]

Despite men's natural vanity they have often needed clever salesmanship to become wearers of hairpieces. Robust-looking salesmen have knocked on selected doors in the evening. They were almost invariably bald. The reason was succinctly explained to a British reporter who answered an advertisement for a sales representative with thinning hair. 'The job is selling wigs,' said the firm's personnel officer, 'and it's very useful if, after half an hour's chat with a possible customer, our men can clinch what they've been saying by removing a wig which the other man had taken for natural hair.'

Since the 1960s the main change in wigmaking has been a greater use of fine synthetic fibre instead of coarse Asian hair. Techniques have not altered except in detail.

Fewer men are ordering toupees in the 1990s, the partially bald head being itself a point of vanity, suggesting brains and distinguished character. For those who insist on artificial hair, with a view perhaps to looking younger, improvements to the double-sided tape, used to keep the wig in place, have made an appearance of perfect reality possible, even when hair is combed back instead of being allowed to tumble over the forehead.

Among the very vain, bonding is still resorted to. This entails attaching artificial hair to the remaining natural hair and looks satisfactory for a short time; it necessitates constant attention by the wigmaker, since natural hair-growth soon makes the deception apparent. Transplanting healthy hair from areas of good growth has commonly been a disappointment, so sparsely does it grow in the new position.

Underneath view of a modern unisex hairpiece, designed to be worn 'either at the crown to give the "sixties" effect or on top to give extra volume'

Modern toupees for men are often slept in and swum in, but a spokeswoman for Carpenter's Wigs of Maidstone says toupees so used look 'pretty gruesome' by the time a fortnightly maintenance visit comes round. Some try to look after their wigs, by putting them through the washing machine and hanging them on the line to dry. However, wigmakers say the washing machine does not necessarily do them much good.

9

Female Towers and Male Embarrassments

In the late eighteenth century wealth came the way of the wigmakers from women choosing, with ludicrous vanity, to have their hair two feet high. To meet the French-inspired fashion, large quantities of false hair were needed.

At first only the hair in front rose, dressed over pads. Then the whole head was widened and built up in a tower, this tower sometimes reaching, in the 1770s, to a height of two feet six inches. The vanity was well recorded in contemporary cartoons, artists noting that Marie Antoinette had to lift off part of her *tête* to enter her carriage.

To achieve the fashionable *tête* there had to be an elaborate framework of padding consisting of greased wool with horsehair. The natural hair was built up on this as far as it would go, plastered down with paste and then supplemented by several times its amount of false hair. A rich woman could well spend half a day with her hairdresser, 'making a head'. Even those unable to command the attentions of a hairdresser struggled to adopt French hair. A newspaper advertisement of 1778 drew attention to a 'new invented Elastic Cushion' which was said to be 'very convenient

There is exaggeration, of course, but in the late eighteenth century some women did in fact have hair up to 2ft 6in high. An elaborate framework was needed, and difficulty arose when entering doorways

venient for ladies that dress their own hair, as it
required but few or no pins'.

Ornaments for the lofty heads of hair included
vegetables, fruits, feathers and baskets of flowers.

Sometimes the flowers were provided with water. 'I wore in my hair,' writes Mme d'Oberkirch in her *Memoirs*, 'little flat bottles shaped to the curvature of the head; into these a little water was poured for the purpose of preserving the freshness of the flowers . . . This did not always succeed, but when it did, the effect was charming.'[1]

In France, some of the hair ornaments were inspired by political events. In 1778, following a sea battle in which the ship *La Belle Poule* successfully engaged the English, women took to crowning their hair with a model of a frigate in full sail complete with cannon and flags.

Even without the need to keep the head upright and not upset the flower water, the inconvenience of wearing tall hair was considerable. A correspondent of the *Lady's Magazine* had this to say in March 1776. 'I have seen several ladies, very handsome, so disguised and features quite distorted, by the horrid drag of their hair to a height absolutely half as tall as themselves, and so loaded with game, flowers, fruit, herbs, ribbons, pins, etc. . . . that it has really seemed a pain for them to move or speak for fear the wonderful building be demolished.'

The caricaturists of the period had no trouble depicting women in ridiculous postures. Looking about them the artists could see, as everyone else could see, that the lady of quality going by in her sedan chair was not sitting in it but squatting on the floor.

The *Gentleman's and London Magazine* reported in 1777 that the seats of coaches were already sunk almost to the bottom, and though women sat with their knees up to the pits of their stomachs, they were still obliged to bend forwards to avoid touching the roof. 'Yet they are not to be talked out of this absurdity. The fashion is likely to last.'

'A Flower Garden' (1770s). The *Pall Mall* liked to ridicule women's fashions, and it was not difficult to do so

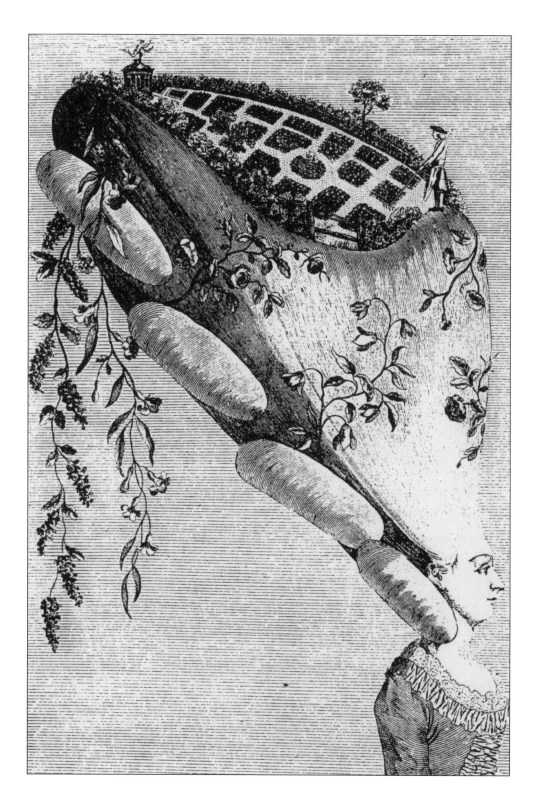

It lasted for a good ten years. Even Nancy Wood-forde, a vicar's niece living in a remote Norfolk village, was dressing her hair in the tall French manner in 1782 – according to Parson Woodforde's reference in his diary to her acquisition of a cushion on which to arrange it.

An impossible absurdity engraved for the *Pall Mall* in the 1770s

Catching fire was more than a remote possibility in times when rooms were lighted with chandeliers holding dozens of candles. The point is brought out by Christopher Anstey in the *New Bath Guide* of 1776:

> Yet Miss at the rooms
> Must beware of her plumes;
> For if Vulcan her feather embraces,

Like poor Lady Laycock
She'll burn like a haycock,
And roast all the Loves and the Graces.

A degree of discomfort was taken for granted, however. Anna Green Winslow, in a diary entry for 1771, referred to the effect of building up her hair on a roll consisting of cow's tail and coarse horsehair: 'It makes my head ache and burn and itch like anything.'[2]

Going to bed was difficult. By sleeping in a propped-up position, a head could be made to last a week; though by that time dismantlement became a matter of urgency. Combing to give elementary hygiene was not possible. In 1767 the Countess of Suffolk heard someone remark to Lord Chesterfield that women at Bath seemed to be wearing their hair 'three or four storeys high'. Lord Chesterfield replied: 'Yes, and I believe every storey is inhabited.'[3]

The ivory or silver scratching stick of the period, with its end in the form of a tiny human hand, was for scratching backs rather than heads: for the latter a simple pin was more practical. Scratching of course was a feeble palliative and many women had their heads shaved and wore complete wigs in the tall style of the day.

Around 1780 women's hair decreased in height but increased in width. The back part was done in a chignon and hung in a flat loop from the top of the head to the shoulders; otherwise it might be plaited. The towering head-dress persisted longer in France than in England. Madame Dubarry wore it, as did everyone at Court, throughout the decade prior to the fall of the Bastille in 1789.

To understand why English women gave themselves to so ridiculous a vanity it is only necessary to remember the strength of French influence and to read of the extreme seriousness with which anything to do with hairdressing was taken in France. From early in the eighteenth century the more dexterous women's hairdressers were idolized; they were spoiled children of the ladies of the Court and of the rich bourgeoisie. They made a lot of money. Theirs was the privilege of kissing brides whose hair they had dressed. Their names – André, François, Jacques, Léonard and Pierre – live on in the salons of Britain.

The power of hairdressers was such that when, in 1776, Louis XVI set about disbanding the guilds of tradesmen, only the guild of perruquiers-coiffeurs remained intact: the national exchequer could not afford the huge sum of money needed for buying back the positions purchased.

One of the famous women's hairdressers was Le Gros. In 1763 he set up in the Place Vendome, Paris, an exhibition of about thirty dolls, each with its hair arranged in one of his styles. These dolls were the forerunners of many others, most of them formed with cardboard, which were to spread fashion ideas throughout Europe.

Le Gros, having become famous, knew how to keep himself in the public eye. He created the *Académie de Coiffure*, the first regular school of hairdressing, and students who completed courses there (women as well as men) were rewarded with medals said to have the value of diplomas.

Models employed for demonstrations at the school had to be extremely pretty; they were known as *preteuses de têtes*, takers of hair arrangements. When *têtes* prepared by students turned out well, Le Gros had the work shown off to the public by a *preteuse de têtes* strolling about the boulevards. But Le Gros did not confine his talents to working with hair; he wrote a well-selling book called *L'Art de la Coiffure des Dames*.

Le Gros's school of hairdressing was soon followed by others, all called *académies*. Hairdressers took to writing above their shop fronts '*Académicien des Coiffures et des Modes*'. Léonard Autier, Le Gros's successor and hairdresser to Marie Antoinette herself, became known as '*le grand Léonard*'. He was responsible for most of the tall and monumental styles here referred to. He emigrated to Russia during the Revolution, but returned to France in 1823 when he was found a job as an undertaker.

The fashion for elaborate *coiffures* died within a few years of the French Revolution getting under way. In 1793 Louis XVI, Marie Antoinette and other aristocrats lost their lives at the guillotine. There reached England in that year a weird fashion, inspired by horrific events, called '*la coiffure à la victime*'. The natural hair was cut short and worn carefully dishevelled and wild. Some went so far in bad taste as to wear with this *coiffure* a crimson ribbon round the neck.

Among other short, seemingly casual, styles for women was the porcupine, in which the hair on the front of the head was made to stand up. There was a fad, too, for hair that was cut within an inch of the scalp; but this one did not last. Many wearers, indeed, soon bought moderate sized wigs called *cache-folies*.

The late James Laver of the V&A points out that just as women's head-dresses were prominent immediately before the French Revolution, so they were prominent again just before the First World War, when everyone wanted a cartwheel hat loaded with birds and flowers. Giving so much prominence to the female head was not only a portent, he writes; it was a protest. 'In their symbolic language the head-dresses

were saying something, and what they were saying was "Votes for Women". After a great social upheaval women permitted themselves very small heads as a sign that some kind of victory had been won.'[4]

Men's wigs became potentially comic at the beginning of the nineteenth century, as suggested in the last chapter, when private people had taken to wearing their own hair cut short. The professional men who still wore wigs – the doctors, clergymen and lawyers – were now subject to amused comment in the event of a mishap. Daniel O'Connell invited a laugh deliberately at an election meeting in Dublin in the 1830s when he lifted his wig to meet an opponent's taunt that without it his head was little to boast of.

Previously a man had thought nothing of allowing his shaved head to be seen from time to time, and if his wig came off unexpectedly he would not be con-

Hatted visitors arrive at Henley Station for the regatta in 1905

ered a figure of fun. The wig of Frederick the Great
fell off one day as he too carelessly raised his hat to
the people while riding through Berlin. He rode on
calmly, ignoring slight laughter. In 1830, on the other
hand, it was very embarrassing for the apothecary of
Robert Seymour's drawing when he lost his wig on
mounting an excitable horse. The accident was wit-
nessed by a party of huntsmen:

> And tho' no cry the huntsmen heard,
> They saw the Doctor – bald!

In the eighteenth century a clergyman staying at a
good inn might quite naturally have handed his wig
to a servant before retiring and asked him for a cloth
night cap. But it is intentionally ridiculous in Combe's
Tours of Doctor Syntax, published in the early nineteenth century, when Doctor Syntax thus commands
an inn servant:

> Go, tell the maid to shew the bed,
> Where I may lay my aching head;
> Here, take my wig, and bring a cap;
> My eyelids languish for a nap . . .

William Combe made the most of his character's wig.
It gets caught on the horns of a cow, and is dislodged
when highwaymen attack him. Once, during a night
at an inn, he is aroused by the rustling noise of the
wig being mauled by a troop of frisking rats. Having
summoned the ostler to get rid of the rats, Dr Syntax
goes to sleep again, not realizing until the morning
that his wig has become utterly unwearable. The landlord is sent for. He enters, bowing, and offers assur-
ances that no such complaint has ever been made
before. Dr Syntax cuts this short:

> Tell me, landlord, does your town
> A skilful peruke-maker own
> Who can this caxon dire restore
> To the same form it had before?

The landlord names the local barber and observes:

> I doubt not, Sire, that to a hair,
> He will your mangled wig repair.

But the man, when he arrives, declares that the wig is beyond mending; all he can do is to offer a second-hand wig. The incident closes – amusingly enough – with Dr Syntax continuing his journey unsuitably dressed in a two-tailed lawyer's wig.[5]

Wigs lingered late among clergymen, who wore them at all times. Bishops were still going about in them during the Reform Bill agitations of 1831 and thereby made themselves easy targets for public annoyance. A bishop who wore his physical bob wig while preaching one Sunday at St Bride's, Fleet Street, was publicly insulted. Largely as a result of this incident, all bishops gave up everyday use of the wigs which made them so conspicuous. Bishop Blomfield, Bishop of London, obtained the permission of William IV for the clergy to be wigless even when sitting as members of the episcopal bench. Archbishop Sumner was the last clergyman to wear a wig of vanity; he is shown with it in a painting by John Phillip of the marriage of the Princess Royal in 1858.

It might be thought that even though the male wig of vanity fell out of use, the wigmakers would have been kept at least reasonably busy covering men's bald patches.

But hardly anyone wanted a 'necessity' wig. Wigs,

like false teeth, were now considered a shameful vanity and almost unmentionable. When advertised in the Press, wigs were euphemistically mentioned directly as a 'gentleman's invisible peruke' or 'gentleman's head of hair'.

An advertisement of 1840 by Ross and Sons of Bishopsgate Street, London, drew attention to 'Invisible Ventilating Perukes', and claimed that these offered 'so close a resemblance to nature as to defy detection'. The firm had a 'large assortment always kept for inspection, any one of which, if approved of, saves the purchaser time and trouble'. People wishing to order by post, without a visit, were invited to send their measurements as follows: 'Round the head in manner of a fillet, leaving the ears loose. From the forehead over to the poll, as deep each way as required. From ear to ear across the forehead, close down to the point level with the whisker.'

For those interested in partial wigs the following measurements were required: 'From the front as far forward as required to the hair behind. From one side to the other across the forehead as far as bald. Across the crown or rise of head.'

Even with the small diagrams supplied, these instructions must have been hard to follow – and the fit of the resultant wig uncertain. But men who wore wigs for baldness in the nineteenth century were at least fortunate in that hair-styles were shaggy; the hair-line was not expected to show, hair could hang down on the forehead, and natural hair partings, always the weak point in a wig, were commonly rudimentary. In theory, at least, wigs should have been less noticeable than when 'short back and sides' became the custom; in practice many of them were absurdly obvious.

The Victorian period proceeded. Even the trade Press could not take men's wigs seriously. During the first thirteen years of the publication of the *Hairdressers' Weekly Journal,* founded in 1882, they were the subject of only half a dozen editorial references, and all of these were either facetious or derogatory. One editorial makes fun of old men with wigs too young for them and with dyed moustaches and whiskers; another seeks to amuse with reflections about a woman's anger at finding that she cannot effectively pull the hair of a wigged husband.

In 1886 the *London Evening News* summed up the situation as follows: 'Wig-wearing outside the theatrical professions is rare, though a few foolish old men, ashamed of being bald, and a few silly old maids, anxious to hide the footsteps of advancing age, give some employment in the manufacture of wigs, patches and fronts.'

In America meanwhile there had been great technical advances. Men could be fitted with wigs they were proud of. The greatest step forward was the introduction in New York in 1867 of fine hair lace, a net made entirely of human hair for use as foundation material. Strips of similar material are still used for the partings of good wigs. The lace allowed the wearer's scalp to show through; and when the hairs, individually selected, were knotted to the mesh, they appeared to be growing naturally. Here was a big improvement on all previous nets for partings; a 'flesh-coloured' net which had caused a stir when introduced in France between 1805 and 1810 looked, by comparison, coarse.

Where expense was no object, New York wigmakers of the mid-nineteenth century turned out superb wigs with foundations made almost wholly of hair lace. The hair could be parted anywhere, like growing hair, to give a parting which looked exactly like a parting on the natural scalp. English and French wigmakers also undertook wigs on bases of hair lace – and some of them bear comparison with the best that can be made today. Records exist to show that the firm of John Stevens of Bristol, for example, had made several wigs of this type by the year 1870; not only was the foundation entirely hair but all the sewing was done with hair. The firm's last hair-only (and incidentally springless) wig was made in 1926 for £50.[6]

The American *Hairdresser and Perfumer* related in 1882 how a young man with a very expensive blonde, hair-lace wig was obliged to take it back to his barber. A chunk of hair was missing. He explained that a girl asked him for a lock of his hair and he had found himself acquiescing. But the girl was gentle with him, he said, and although she cut off the lock close to the head, she did not notice that he was wearing a wig. The barber-wigmaker would not restore the wig all at once. He spread the task over a period, imitating the natural growth by means of short pieces of hair which were exchanged from time to time for longer pieces. The girl did not find out that the young man was bald until after they were married.

By the 1890s a man with money had no great difficulty in being fitted with a brilliantly executed wig; he feared, though, society's scarcely lessened disdain for the idea of men in wigs. The *Hairdressers' Weekly Journal* at last, in 1895, permitted itself some cheerful remarks:

As false teeth are now no longer a source of reproach amongst us, so universal is their use, neither will false hair in the near future tempt the finger of the scorner, so absolutely necessary will it become to most of us . . . Why should not the wig be as recognized a necessity as false teeth or spectacles? If it were a ludicrous caricature of nature, we could understand the popular aversion to it, but this it no longer is.

The paper went on to suggest that in a changeable climate it was important for bald heads to have a covering – and what more natural than the hair which ought to be there? The final argument in favour of 'the modern wig' was that its manufacture gave employment to a 'vast amount of female labour, all the more delicate parts being done by women'. The rosier hopes of the trade were dashed, however, in the early twentieth century, when it became the fashion for men to brush their hair straight back from the hairline.

How much things have changed since then, and how rare is the detectable toupee! Baldness is thought distinguished. Abundant hair is either close shorn or made by young people to look arresting – very long in the 1960s, dyed in bright colours in the 1970s, permed in the 1980s and long once again in the 1990s. No wonder so many wigmakers advertise.

10

High Heels, Fans and Hats

Boots and shoes have lent themselves for centuries to pleasing a person's vanity, especially the heels and toes. Heels have gone up and gone down. Toes have been dead square, pointed and even sprung to resemble sleigh runners (Mark Twain suggested in *Tom Sawyer* that nineteenth-century shoes were so formed by 'young men sitting with their feet against a wall for hours together').

Heels were apparently introduced in the 1590s and were from one to two inches high for both sexes. But men worried about their shortness would contrive to add to their height. Tobias Smollett writes of an eighteenth-century character that 'the heels of his shoes were so high as to raise his feet three inches at least'. And June Swann, in her book, *Shoes*, relates that a man's black satin shoe in the Whitby Museum has a six-inch heel.[1]

Men and women of the eighteenth century liked red heels, especially for their boots. Yellow heels were, however, esteemed by men going to the seaside, according to the *London Chronicle* of 1787. The flimsy French or Pompadour heel had now become admired and a book called *Receipt for Modern Dress* advises ladies to

A man's black satin shoes with six-inch heels, dating from the early nineteenth century

> Mount on French heels when you go to a ball
> 'Tis the fashion to totter and show you can fall.

In another rhyme Francis Fawkes writes in *His Mistress's Picture* (1755), that women looked silly

> Mounted high and buckled low
> Tottering every step they go.

Some heels have been chunky, as in Georgian times, and others absurdly thin, made of wood under fabric and ending in a metal spike to avoid too frequent breakage like the modern stiletto heel. The latter heels were of course impractical for walking on cobblestones. High heels disappeared in France after the Revolution but came back when men complained that they needed a space for anchoring the trouser strap. A few extra high heels were made for dandies in the

1830s, but by the '40s such male heels had disappeared.

In the 1850s there was a further reappearance of the high heel for women and *The Ladies' Treasury* observed in 1868 that high-heeled boots for women were universal 'notwithstanding that medical men have been writing very severely against them, saying the fashion causes corns, cramps and lameness'. Men's heels of the late nineteenth century were normally one and a quarter inches high, whether on shoes or boots, and so they continued into the twentieth century. The fashionable heel for women became a height of two to two and a half inches.

It was not until the late 1960s that men took to wearing noticeably high heels again, the first time since the 1720s. This was the era of the stacked heel and platform sole for both men and women.

A man's platform sole shoe, from the 1970s

The toes of shoes have gone through as many fickle changes of fashion as heels. The long square toe came in with Charles II on his return from France. Some toes were turned up like a hook. It was mostly men who wore footwear of this sort, women preferring a slightly pointed toe flat on the ground – until the 1760s when an oval shape became usual. The extended square toe, though resisted by many men, came back around 1830 with a spring to make it rise up. Women took to similar shapes, shallow and most uncomfortable, and the publication *Handbook of the Toilet*, 1841, comments: 'There hardly exists an Englishwoman whose toes are not folded over one another, each of these crooked and the nails destroyed, such were women's sufferings for vanity.'

Noticeable deformities came with the thorough-going pointed shoe of the 1860s, and *The English Woman's Domestic Magazine* only half jokingly suggested amputation of one or more toes to wear the latest tiny shoes from Paris. However, by 1881 the *Boot and Shoe Trade Journal* was able to report that uncomfortably pointed shoes represented a dying fashion. The pointed toe has lasted, of course, but nowadays the design takes at least some account of the foot's natural shape.[2]

Shoes were by no means the only accessories available to appease a woman's vanity: the folding fan, beautifully made and usually decorative, is clearly much more than just an instrument for causing a breeze. A fan was meant to compliment the bearer, to enable her to flirt over the top, concealing those parts of her face she did not wish studied – especially perhaps the mouth when she was smiling broadly.'[3] Fans had been popular since Roman times and Queen Elizabeth I had hundreds. People frequently made gifts of them to her, and from all the Queen's portraits

No. 2. FASHIONABLE FANS.

it can be seen that the fan was an accessory enhancing the beauty of her hands.

In the seventeenth century fans became an integral part of the trousseau of the fashionable bride. The two main kinds of folding fan are the pleated and the *brisé*. The pleated fan is a shaped leaf placed over a set of sticks; the base of the sticks may be rounded off or shaped and there is of course a pivot to permit articulation. The *brisé* fan consists of sticks only, held together at the top by a ribbon and tapering to the pivot at the base.

In the eighteenth century rich girls received much instruction in deportment from a dancing master and this included correct management of the fan. One handbook had this to say: 'The fan is genteel and useful, therefore it is proper that young ladies should know how to make a genteel and proper use of it. In order that they may do so, I have pointed out six positions of the fan, genteel and very becoming.'[4]

An article from *The Queen*, 1887. How a woman managed her fan could determine, it was said, her social class. A fan could be made to hide parts of the face a woman did not wish to have stared at

Perpetual fluttering of the fan was considered absurd in nineteenth-century handbooks, but restrained use enabled the adroit woman to bring out comments in conversation and to an extent there was a language of the fan.

How a woman managed her fan could determine, it was said, her social class. 'Women are armed with fans,' wrote a *Spectator* correspondent in 1711, 'as men are with swords.'

Fans continued to be manufactured well into the twentieth century and in 1928 the bride of the young King Farouk of Egypt was seen in official pictures holding a splendid example encrusted with diamonds. In the hot summer of 1983 several women were photographed carrying fans at a royal garden party in London.[5]

And what about hats? The numerous kinds available for each sex perhaps belong more to the realm of fashion than to vanity.[6]

Over the years fashion has provided the man with a wide choice of headgear: tricorns, bowlers, toppers, panamas, boaters and pork pies. It was perhaps not his particular choice to wear them, but fashion dictated. Vanity only really arose in the way some wore their conventional hats; pushed back or tilted to one side, both adjustments causing a marked change in appearance.

It is true, though, that in late Victorian times there was lasting class-consciousness over men's obligatory hats. Flora Thompson, describing villagers going to church in the 1880s, noted that 'the squire and the farmer wore top hats and the squire's head gardener and the schoolmaster and the village carpenter. The farm labourers wore bowlers and the older men soft round black felts.'[7]

An exploratory style in hats for 1924 – Paquin's fashion

Vanity was undoubtedly at the root of the fashion for the black bowler associated with the City (it was originally agricultural headgear), which caused numerous men unconnected with the City of London to wear it. In the 1920s and '30s the bowler took on the role of the hat for the aspiring man. Charlie Chaplin caricatured the pretensions of these men in his films.[8]

Today the common custom is to be hatless and vanity in headgear is remarkable only for its absence. On special occasions too, such as when a young man hires a top hat for his wedding, but it falls too low over his ears, it is his lack of ease rather then his vanity which is obvious. Edward VIII, one of the no-hat brigade, except when hatters obliged him to try their hats, would certainly have approved.

Charlie Chaplin made fun of the City gent with his bowler hat, in the 1920s

Notes

Introduction

1. Richmal Crompton, *William the Showman*, Newnes, 1937
2. Edward Gibbon, *Decline and Fall of the Roman Empire*, *c.* 1780. From an abridgement, Chatto, 1960
3. Thelma Chapman, *Victorian Life in Photographs*, Book Club Associates, 1974
4. Candida McWilliam, *Vogue*, 1990
5. Albert Speer, *Inside the Third Reich*, Weidenfeld and Nicolson, 1971
6. Anthony Trollope, *Barchester Towers*, Oxford, 1857
7. Alex Walker, *Evening Standard*, 1990
8. William Congreve, *The Way of the World*, 1700
9. Antonia Fraser, *The Weaker Vessel*, Weidenfeld and Nicolson, 1984
10. Harold Nicolson, *Diaries and Letters*, Collins, 1967
11. John Woodforde, *The Strange Story of False Teeth*, Routledge, 1968
12. Dinah Hall, *Independent Sunday Review*, 1991

Chapter 1

1. Frances Wood, *A Companion to China*, Weidenfeld and Nicolson, 1988
2. Wood, op. cit.
3. Geoffrey Chaucer, *Canterbury Tales*, 'The Parson's Tale'

4. Diana de Marly, *Fashion for Men*, Batsford, 1985

5. Eline Canter Cremers, *The Agony of Fashion*, Blandford, 1980

6. de Marly, op. cit.

7. Christopher Hibbert, *The English*, Book Club Associates, 1987

8. Hibbert, op. cit.

9. Canter Cremers, op. cit.

10. Antonia Fraser, *The Weaker Vessel*, Weidenfeld and Nicolson, 1984

11. Canter Cremers, op. cit.

Chapter 2

1. Anthony Wallace, *The Progress of Plastic Surgery*, Oxford, W.A. Meeuws, 1982

2. John Mulliken, 'Charles Conrad Miller', *Plastic and Reconstructive Surgery*, 1977

3. S.J. Perelman, *The Best of S.J. Perelman*, New York Modern Library, 1947

4. B.O. Rogers, *A History of Cosmetic Surgery*, New York Academy of Medicine, 1971

5. Eline Canter Cremers, *The Agony of Fashion*, Blandford, 1980

Chapter 3

1. Julian Critchley, *The Independent*, 1991

2. Luigi Barzini, *The Italians*, Hamish Hamilton, 1964

3. Richmal Crompton, *William the Good*, Newnes, 1928

4. Geoffrey Chaucer, *The Canterbury Tales*, 'Prologue'

5. Harold Nicolson, *Good Behaviour*, Constable, 1955

6. Nancy Mitford, *Nobesse Oblige*, Hamilton, 1956

Chapter 4

1. James Boswell, *Journal of a Tour to the Hebrides*, London, 1785

2. Prince Pückler-Muskau, *Tour of England*, 1832, quoted by D.M. George, *Social Satire*, Lane, 1967

3. Ellen Moers, *The Dandy, Brummell to Beerbohm*, Secker and Warburg, 1960

4. Gillian Avery, *Nineteenth-century Children*, Hodder and Stoughton, 1965

5. Harold Nicolson, *Good Behaviour*, Constable, 1955

6. Fenja Gunn, *The Artificial Face*, David and Charles, 1973

7. William Thackeray, *Vanity Fair*, Nelson, 1848

8. Rosina Harrison, *My Life in Service,* 1930, quoted by Mark Girouard

Chapter 5

1. Lawrence Wright, *Clean and Decent*, Routledge, 1960

2. Elizabeth Burton, *The Georgians at Home*, Longman, 1967

3. Fenja Gunn, *The Artificial Face*, 1973

4. Christopher Hibbert, *The English*, Book Club Associates, 1987

5. William Cobbett, *Advice to a Lover*, London, 1829

Chapter 6

1. Vincenzo Guerini, *A History of Dentistry*, Lea and Febiger, Philadelphia, 1909

2. Robert Herrick, epigram *'Upon Glasco'*

3. John Gray, *Preservation of the Teeth*, R. and J. Taylor, 1838

4. Mrs Delaney, *Life and Correspondence*, London, 1861

5. John Tomes, *The Management of Artificial Teeth*, Parker, 1851

6. Pièrre Fauchard, *Le Chirurgien Dentiste*, Mariette, Paris, 1728

7. Eleaser Gidney, *Treatise on the Teeth*, Augustine Dauby, Utica, 1824

Chapter 7

1. John Hunter, *Natural History of the Human Teeth*, Johnson, 1778
2. Thomas Berdmore, *Disorders and Deformities of the Teeth*, Exshaw, Dublin, 1769
3. John Gray, *Preservation of the Teeth*, Taylor, 1838
4. J. Menzies Campbell, *Dentistry Then and Now*, privately printed, Glasgow, 1963
5. Menzies Campbell, op. cit.

Chapter 8

1. Alfred Lucas, *Ancient Egyptian Materials and Industries*, London, 1934
2. Jean Baptiste Thiers, *Histoire des Peruques*, Paris, 1690
3. James Stevens Cox, *Dictionary of Hairdressing and Wigmaking*, Hairdressers' Technical Council, 1966
4. Gladys Scott Thomson, *Life in a Noble Household*, 1937
5. Stevens Cox, op. cit.
6. Macdonald, op. cit.
7. Stevens Cox, op. cit.

Chapter 9

1. C.W. and Phyllis Cunnington, *English Costume in the Eighteenth Century*, Faber and Faber, 1955
2. Cunnington, op. cit.
3. James Stevens Cox, *Dictionary of Hairdressing and Wigmaking*, Hairdressers' Technical Council, 1966
4. James Laver, *Clothes*, Burke, 1952
5. William Combe, *Tours of Dr Syntax*, 1920, Warne
6. Stevens Cox, op. cit.

Chapter 10

1. June Swann, *Shoes*, Batsford, 1982
2. Swann, op. cit.
3. Hélène Alexander, *Fans*, Batsford, 1984
4. *The Young Gentleman and Lady's Private Tutor*, 1771, quoted by Hélène Alexander
5. Alexander, op. cit.
6. Fiona Clark, *Hats*, Batsford, 1982
7. Flora Thompson, *Lark Rise to Candleford*, Oxford, 1945
8. Clark, op. cit.

Sources

Unless otherwise stated the place of publication is London.

Alexander, Hélène, *Fans*, Batsford, 1984

Asser, Joyce, *Historic Hairdressing*, Pitman, 1966

Avery, Gillian, *Nineteenth-Century Children*, Hodder and Stoughton, 1965

Barzini, Luigi, *The Italians*, Hamish Hamilton, 1964

Bird, Penelope, *The Male Image*, Batsford, 1979

Bloom, Barbara, *The Reign of Narcissism*, Serpentine Gallery, London, 1990

Bly, Robert, *Iron John*, Element, 1990

Bremner, M., *The Story of Dentistry*, Kimpton, 1946

Bulwer-Lytton, Edward, *Pelham or The Adventures of a Gentleman*, R.E. King, 1828

Burton, Elizabeth, *The Georgians at Home*, Longman 1967

—— , *The Elizabethans at Home*, Longman

—— , *The Jacobeans at Home*, Longman

Canter Cremers, Eline, *The Agony of Fashion*, Blandford, 1980

Chesterfield, Fourth Earl of, *Letters to His Son*, 1774, Dent

Clark, Fiona, *Hats*, Batsford, 1984

Combe, William, *Doctor Syntax in Search of Consolation*, London, 1820, Frederick Warne

Cunnington, C.W. and Phyllis, *English Costume in The Seventeenth Century*, Faber and Faber, 1955

Dacatur, Stephen, *The Private Affairs of George Washington*, New York, 1933

de Chemant, Dubois, *A Dissertation on Artificial Teeth*, Barker, 1797

de Marly, Diana, *Fashion for Men*, Batsford, 1985

Ewing, Elizabeth, *A History of Twentieth-century Fashion*, Batsford, 1974

Fraser, Antonia, *The Weaker Vessel*, Weidenfeld and Nicolson, 1984

Gidney, Eleazer, *Treatise on the Teeth*, Augustine Danby, Utica, 1824

Gray, John, *Preservation of the Teeth*, Taylor, 1838

Guerini, Vincenzo, *A History of Dentistry*, Lea and Febiger, Philadelphia, 1909

Gunn, Fenja, *The Artificial Face*, David and Charles, 1973

Hibbert, Christopher, *The English*, Book Club Associates with Grafton, 1984

Laver, James, *The Age of Optimism*, Weidenfeld and Nicolson, 1966

Lord, Shirley, *You are Beautiful*, Sidgwick and Jackson, 1978

Lufkin, Arthur, *A History of Dentistry*, Kimpton, 1948

Macdonald, John, *Memoirs of an Eighteenth-century Footman*, Routledge, 1927

Menzies Campbell, J., *Dentistry Then and Now*, privately printed in Glasgow, 1963

Mitford, Nancy, *Noblesse Oblige*, Hamilton, 1956

Moers, Ellen, *The Dandy, Brummell to Beerbohm*, Secker and Warburg, 1960

Moneypenny and Buckle, *Life of Disraeli*, John Murray, 1929

Mortimer, W., *Essay on Artificial Teeth*, Samuel Highley, 1845

Nicolson, Harold, *Good Behaviour*, Constable, 1955

Nunn, Joan, *Fashion in Costume 1200–1980*, Herbert Press, 1984

Pass, Horatio, *Artificial Teeth and Palates*, Churchill, 1846

Piper, David, *The English Face*, Thames and Hudson, 1957

Renoir, J., *My Father*, London, 1958

Saunders, Edwin, *Mineral Teeth*, Renshaw, 1841

Scott Thomson, Gladys, *Life in a Noble Household*, Cape, 1937

Smith, Maurice, *A Short History of Dentistry*, Wingate, 1958

Stevens Cox, J., *Dictionary of Hairdressing and Wigmaking*, Hairdressers' Technical Council, 1966

Swann, June, *Shoes*, Batsford, 1982

Thackeray, William, *Vanity Fair*, Nelson, 1848

Tomes, John, *The Management of Artificial Teeth*, Parker, 1851

Wallace, Anthony, *The Progress of Plastic Surgery*, W.A. Meeus, 1982

Weinberger, B.H., *History of Dentistry in America*, Mosby, St Louis, 1948

Wood, Frances, *A Companion to China*, Weidenfeld and Nicolson, 1988

Woodforde, James, *Diary for 1764*, Oxford, 1924

Woodforde, John, *The Strange Story of False Teeth*, Routledge, 1968

—— *The Strange Story of False Hair*, Routledge, 1971

Wright, Lawrence, *Clean and Decent*, Routledge, 1960

Index